MW01679865

I hope this book will help you + Leland Always remember to love each other.

With Love Always,

Momma

2/14/94

When Growing Up Hurts Too Much

A Parent's Guide to Knowing When and How to Choose a Therapist with Your Teenager

SCOTT O. HARRIS, Ph.D.

EDWARD N. REYNOLDS, Ph. D.

Lexington Books

D.C. Heath and Company • Lexington, Massachusetts • Toronto

Library of Congress Cataloging-in-Publication Data

Harris, Scott O.
When growing up hurts too much : a parent's guide to knowing when and how to choose a therapist with your teenager / Scott O. Harris, Edward N. Reynolds.
p. cm.
Includes bibliographical references (p.) and index.
ISBN 0-669-24316-7 (alk. paper)
1. Adolescent psychopathology—Popular works. 2. Adolescent psychotherapy—Popular works. I. Reynolds, Edward N. II. Title.
RJ499.H3925 1990
616.89'022—dc20 90-6151
CIP

Published simultaneously in Canada
Printed in the United States of America
Casebound International Standard Book Number: 0-669-24316-7
Library of Congress Catalog Card Number: 90-6151

The paper used in this publication meets the minimum requirements of American National Standard for Information Sciences—Permanence of Paper for Printed Library Materials, ANSI Z39.48-1984.

Year and number of this printing

90 91 92 8 7 6 5 4 3 2 1

This book is dedicated to our teenage clients and their parents. They have helped us understand, in terms more profound than any text could ever teach, that the joy of growth outweighs its pain.

I'd like to acknowledge my family for their love and support, and to remember my father, Bud Harris.

— Scott O. Harris, Ph.D.

To my family, with gratitude for their help and encouragement.

— Edward N. Reynolds, Ph.D.

Contents

Foreword

Bill Cosby

THREE Cosby offspring have journeyed through adolescence and achieved young adulthood; the remaining two are in separate stages of their teen years. At first Camille, my wife, and I tended to feel that we could manage every problem on our own, that asking for help was a reflection of weakness or ignorance on our part. But along the way we overcame our reluctance and sought guidance from therapists and teachers to help our children cope with problems they encountered during trying periods.

I know, from my associations with friends and colleagues, that strong resistance to and lack of understanding about seeking assistance for adolescents is still prevalent. In my opinion, this attitude relates to the commonly held belief that youngsters in this age group merely experience turbulent emotions that will automatically sort themselves out in time. As a result, many parents stand by helplessly as a child disintegrates, refusing to consult a therapist; others wait too long to seek help from a professional, thereby prolonging the pain and possibly jeopardizing the realization of a positive outcome.

There are too many stereotypes about the troubled teen years, so I am pleased to report that the authors of this book avoid the error of treating adolescence as just a difficult and painful period. Parents know that adolescence does not suddenly materialize from a psychological and social vacuum. It evolves from both the good and bad experiences that affect children in their early years.

The suggestions in these pages are not buried in psychological babble, but are clear, simple, and specific, offering important tips on parenting for a critical stage of development. The book contains valuable information about what is normal and what is pathological about various forms of adolescent behavior and how to cope with them.

For example, some teenagers may rebel at parents' tough and unbending requirements for absolute obedience. In such a situation a modification of parenting style may be effective. Parents must learn to unbend to some extent and to discover, as I did, that the teen years demand the maximum amount of parental flexibility and patience.

Young people cannot be pigeonholed by age or stage. I found, among our own children, that some became independent at an earlier age than others. In the real world, some teens drop out of high school to go to work, others graduate and go to work—and some who do not graduate remain unemployed. Then there are those who go on to college, to drop out or to graduate. Parents must realize that these categories include many adolescents who are late bloomers. A significant number of youngsters who seriously founder early on significantly achieve at a later age.

It is clear to me that all parents, from all backgrounds, can benefit from the advice this book offers: when and how to choose a therapist with your youngster. Parents whose adolescents are experiencing significant difficulties should find this volume particularly enlightening. The ultimate beneficiaries will be the teenagers who receive help, support, counseling, and psychotherapy from competent and qualified therapists. The worlds of these young people can not only be saved, they can be opened to a bright and hopeful future.

—June 5, 1990

Preface

THIS book is for parents. Specifically, it is for parents facing the challenges and demands of helping their youngsters through the adolescent years—roughly ages twelve through eighteen. While it can be thrilling to watch the growth of self-esteem and independence of late adolescence, the drive toward adulthood can also be fraught with difficulties. Fueled by hormonal changes and guided by society's demand that teens learn to separate from the family and develop an individual identity, the teenage years can be rocky at best.

The emergence of the growing field of family therapy has taught us that what affects one family member affects all. Like the ripples on a lake when a stone is dropped into the water, the stresses and worries of the teenager reverberate throughout the entire family system. Sometimes the reverberation is the normal, inevitable, and necessary stress of change; sometimes the circles in the water become so intense and distorted that they reflect problems below the surface, which require deeper attention.

The goal of this book is twofold. Initially, it aims at helping parents and their teens differentiate between family problems that are normal for everyone and those that are serious enough to require special attention. The second goal of this book is to help parents and their teenagers determine what kinds of help are available and how they can make the wisest choices in finding the professional assistance they require.

Finally, this is meant to be a book of hope and support for teens and their parents as they navigate adolescence together.

Acknowledgment

WITHOUT the expert assistance of Susan Victoria Benford, this book would never have seen the light of day. As a writer, she lightened our too often formal and pedantic style. As an editor, she made accessible our sometimes earth-bound prose. And as an adviser, she brought to the entire project her delightful warmth and enthusiasm—the "Noonie touch"—which gave it a very human heart.

When Growing Up Hurts Too Much

1

Do You Need This Book?

Is your adolescent failing in school despite average or above average intelligence?

Does your teenager seem so severely depressed at times that you think he or she might be considering suicide?

Is your youngster having problems because of drugs and/or alcohol?

Is your adolescent destructive of property or physically violent?

Has your teen been arrested?

Is your youngster isolated or withdrawn most of the time?

Does your adolescent seem paralyzed by the normal stress of everyday life?

Do you suspect that your youngster may be suffering from an eating disorder?

Is your teen's behavior often out of control?

Does your teen often seem dangerous to him- or herself?

Do you fear that your teen may be dangerous to others, including you or other family members?

Are you concerned that your teen may be sexually promiscuous, risking pregnancy?

Are you fearful that your adolescent may be putting him- or herself at risk for sexually transmitted diseases, including AIDS?

The teen years offer a wealth of joy and personal growth for both adolescents and their parents. At last you can talk with your youngster about adult issues such as world events and trends in culture with some satisfaction. And you can share such concerns as the condition of the environment and the outcome of a recent election.

During this period, teens sometimes move toward true friendship with their parents. They share the bonds not only of blood but of common experience, history, and battles fought and won. You know that wonderful feeling of pride and amazement when your youngster has become a more interesting, independent thinker with the beginnings of his or her own worldview.

You see specific growth, a budding sense of self, free thought and expression, and realize that your child is becoming an adult.

Besides being exhilarating, the road through adolescence can be winding, steep, and unpredictable for teenagers and their parents. If you answered "yes" to any of the questions at the beginning of this chapter, you may have a teen who has temporarily lost his or her way. To travel successfully through the teen years, youngsters need adult direction, even though they often resent and seem to reject it. Sometimes they may also need professional guidance.

This book highlights landmarks of adolescent behavior for both teen and parents. It also points to dangerous detours to be aware of. In addition, it can help you determine whether your family needs some professional help to accompany it for a leg of this sometimes precarious journey.

Whether you're trying to catch a youngster who is falling, or pull him or her back from cliff's edge, there will be times when you worry about your teenager. You hope he or she will "come out of this phase" all right. But in some cases, neither hope nor time can heal all the wounds of adolescence. And that is when you might need to turn to psychotherapy.

We will help you determine when your teen's "odd" behavior is essentially normal. We will also give you guidelines to help you discern when your adolescent might need professional help. You'll learn some of the major danger signs to watch for in your teen's actions, mood, and communication. And should your teen's behavior swing out of bounds, you'll be able to turn to this map and see what road to take next.

Though the adolescent years constitute only a fraction of a person's life, they are formative and can be volatile. You and your adolescent may already have encountered some of the obstacles that make this journey especially challenging. Your teen experiences many conflicts. With the conflict set in motion by profound physical changes, most teens struggle with wanting the relative safety of childhood, and the freedom and independence of adulthood. For example:

> Thirteen-year-old Tim gets "creamed" in a soccer game. His parents, who are watching, want to comfort him. Even though he feels like crying, he holds his pain inside, fearing he might look like a wimp to his teammates and might embarrass himself.

As psychologists who work with parents and teens, we will try to address many of the fears parents face during this time:

What is normal?

What is not normal?

How can I discern when my youngster's behavior becomes problematic?

Should my family need assistance, what kinds of help are available?

How can I find the right professional to help my family?

What can I expect from the therapeutic experience?

How can my youngster and I work through our difficulties and start liking each other again?

First, rest assured that, as the parent of an adolescent in crisis, you are not alone. The fact that you picked up this book undoubtedly means that you care about your youngster's future. And you're ready to make the kinds of changes that can help your whole family through this challenging phase.

Become a Savvy Consumer of Psychological Services

Walk down the aisles of any bookstore and you'll run into a large section on consumer education. These books give tips on what to look for in a car, microwave, or dishwasher—as well as what "lemons" to avoid. Consumers pore over this information and comparison shop for hours before making a purchase.

As a consumer of psychological services, you have even more of a right to ask questions and find out what you're getting for your money and your time. Too often in looking for a therapist for an adolescent or family member, parents proceed at their own risk. By being informed and educated, you can greatly increase the chances that you will find the right kind of therapist to help you through this rough time.

Much as you might spend time interviewing pediatricians to find the best match, you should take the time to be sure that the therapist who treats your youngster meets his or her needs. This book will arm you with the right questions to ask. By giving you insights into what to look for in a professional, we hope to guide you toward making a well-informed choice in this crucial decision.

Crossing the Bridge between Childhood and Adulthood

Adolescence is a transition between childhood and adulthood—a sort of limbo in which there seem to be more unknowns than knowns. In our practices, we often see teens wrestle with tough and painful questions:

"What will my body do next?"

"Am I a kid or a grown-up?"

"Do my friends really like me?"

"Am I attractive to the opposite sex?"

"Why is everything so confusing?"

"Is everybody this scared of what the future will bring?"

"Will I ever be successful?"

Like you, we try to guide teens to find the best answers for themselves, and give them the tools they need to face the challenges that will continue to come up in their lives. We also make teens feel that they are understood. In therapy we help teens explore, layer by layer, how they feel about their lives, family, and friends by expressing these feelings to help discover solutions.

Besides "fixing a problem," family or individual therapy can help build your teen's self-esteem at a time when it may be at rock bottom. Working with a psychotherapist reaffirms for your teen that he or she is a good person with reasonable thoughts and feelings, and that he or she is essentially "okay." A therapist can help your teen reveal, explore, and overcome fears and anxieties about growing up, being on his or her own, relating to the opposite sex, and facing his or her own inadequacies.

It is important to remember that a therapist works in tandem with parents. Unlike parents, though, a therapist can give your family an idea of what is normal to expect and can offer suggestions for how you might best cope with the problems at hand. A therapist can serve as an impartial third party to mediate conflicts between you and your teen. He or she can help a teen interpret a world that may not make sense. And a therapist can serve as a translator between you and your teen, to help work through interfering emotions and get to the heart of any issue.

In times of crisis, your therapist can give support to the entire family, and can alleviate any guilt, anxiety, and worry you may experience over your youngster's situation. And he or she can observe from the outside and help you better understand your youngster's patterns of behavior. A therapist can ally with your teen and help the youngster make the difficult crossing from one developmental stage into the next.

A Time of Intense Change

You are traveling the rough road of the teen years—a sometimes difficult, stress-packed time for you and your youngster. Adolescence is a phase of intense physical, emotional, and social change. Moving from junior high to high school, starting to make an emotional break from the family, and beginning to date are a few of the major factors that often spark feelings of frustration, as your teen tests your authority and his or her limits.

On one hand, your youngster loves you and must still rely on you since adult independence has not been achieved. On the other hand, he or she may resent you because you represent boundaries and oppression. This dichotomy can bring tears, anger, and extreme behavior that can make it seem as though your teen is completely confused. Tony is one such case.

> Sixteen-year-old Tony is arrested for drunk driving. When his parents are called, they express shock at his action. Through their tears, they cry that they raised a nice young man, not a criminal. "We started to lose control of him last year," they say. "He seems like a stranger. We don't know what to do."

Even when behavior detours, teens should not be labeled as "bad." A teen who's been "lost in the shuffle" or who's "fallen through the cracks" may be someone with whom no one has made a connection, which is vital to successful development. Adolescent crime, gang violence, and drug abuse, for instance, may reflect earlier neglect or abuse. In many cases underlying problems are more subtle.

Connecting with Your Teenager

Through a combination of nurturing, consistency, and limit-setting, you can help establish that all-important connection with your teen. If Tony's parents had done that earlier, perhaps things would have turned out differently.

While your teen is still in the early warning stages of trouble, you have time to make that connection. When doing so is difficult, a therapist can help your youngster get in touch with his or her feelings—of anger, fear, frustration, and inadequacy—and be free to reconnect with you.

When Problems Aren't Fixed

Bobby had been depressed for eight months. He began idealizing death and identifying with several rock and film stars who had committed suicide at a young age. His parents suspected he had some problems with alcohol. One night he drank an entire bottle of rum, went for a drive, and wrecked the car in a near-fatal accident.

Erik liked to drive his sports car fast through the canyons near his high school. Several times he got drunk at parties, and his friends pleaded with him to let them drive him home. After a homecoming party he was driving his car and ran into an eight-year-old boy on a bicycle, killing him instantly.

Melissa, sixteen, was just beginning to date and was quite shy with boys her age. When Ron, a high school junior she liked very much, told her she would be beautiful if she lost a couple of pounds, she began using laxatives on a daily basis. Soon she was taking twenty pills a day. During a routine physical exam, her family doctor noted a number of potentially dangerous abnormalities resulting from the laxative abuse and notified her parents.

Parents of teens often feel they couldn't have done anything to prevent the problems that befell their youngsters. But in many cases intervention—the right help at the right time—can make an important difference in a teen's life.

Recognize that all youngsters are starving to belong to something. Some fall into gangs. A teen who gets arrested for buying crack might have been looking for leadership he didn't get at home. There may be a difference between two youngsters who sit alone in their rooms listening to music. One may be going through "a phase"; the other could be clinically depressed and desperately in need of intervention. Open your eyes to what your child is showing you, and he or she will have a better chance than if you relied on blind faith.

Let's face it, you once felt you knew your youngster inside and out. His developing personality was as natural to you as your own heartbeat. Now perhaps at times your "baby" seems like a total stranger. His behavior is unpredictable—even frightening. How much of this is to be expected? And when is it time to be concerned? Sometimes the signs can be very clear:

> Sixteen-year-old Rob got *A*s and *B*s in junior high. Now he is failing in school, takes no interest in his studies, and is late for class every day. He no longer wants to participate in family activities. He's belligerent with his parents, especially his father.
>
> Rob frequently sneaks out at night; and hangs out with kids who are truant and involved with drugs. His parents and the school counselor suspect that Rob is becoming involved with drugs. Episodes of misbehavior have become routine. Rob's parents feel as out of control as their son's behavior.

> Fourteen-year-old Marty, who does fairly well in school and has caused few problems for his parents, is suddenly picked up by the police for breaking and entering. He has broken into the school and severely damaged school property. His parents are dismayed.

By using the guidelines in this book, you will learn to recognize your teen's silent cries for help and detect when it may be time to get outside help. As a parent you cannot expect to be everything to your child. Seeking the help of a mental health professional is not a sign of weakness but of strength and courage. In later chapters we will delve into the various types of therapy available and how to select the best professional for you and your adolescent. When the going gets especially tough, keep in mind that the problems of adolescence don't last forever. It only seems that way.

2

Surviving Life with a Teenager

What Is Normal?

Does your teen seem more moody than he or she used to?

Does your teen confide in you less?

Do you sometimes feel that your teen makes excuses to get out of attending family functions?

Does it ever seem as if your teen is embarrassed to be seen with you?

Do you and your teen have frequent arguments about the way he or she is dressed to go out?

Has your youngster started using profanity?

Do you suspect your teen's behavior is normal but want some reassurance?

Ever wonder if those people you see in the monster movies running from their homes shrieking and tearing out their hair are not actors at all—but parents? When the child you have nurtured, loved, and cared for over the last dozen or so years hits adolescence, it can seem that overnight he or she assumes the personality of "The Teen that Ate Tokyo."

Everyone reassures you that what your youngster is going

through is "perfectly normal." Fellow parents relate their own horror stories and try to give solace:

> "All kids go through that rebellious phase."
>
> "You just have to wait it out."
>
> "This awkward stage seems like it's never going to end—but it will."
>
> "A lot of teens dye their hair green and pierce their noses."
>
> "Don't try to understand teens; sometimes the way they behave just doesn't make sense."

In fact, many mental-health professionals believe that, if judged by adult standards, adolescent behavior looks very different from that of adults. Adolescence is a separate phase from both childhood and adulthood.

The wondrous, painful process of adolescent development is ushered forth by physical, emotional, and social changes that take place. While it is a given that these changes may temporarily force your teen off kilter, as a parent you may find some definition of the range of "normal" behavior useful and reassuring.

Your teen may not develop at exactly the same rate as others. Having a general idea of what to expect may prevent you from worrying unnecessarily or from trying to get help for a teen who doesn't need it.

Becoming familiar with the normal stages of adolescence may also help alert you to your youngster's distress call, so that he or she can get needed assistance to weather a particularly stormy time.

Learning to Distinguish between Normal and Abnormal

Pinning down what's normal for a teen can seem like trying to nail Jell-O to the wall. The spectrum of a teen's behavior is broad, and individual behavior changes from month to month—even day to day. Abnormal behavior may show up in one symptom or several. Or there could be a pattern.

It's natural for a teen to want time to himself. But a youngster who begins isolating him- or herself from family, friends, and teachers is showing an unnatural pattern. A youngster's grades may slip in one class. But if she fails in another, and then another, and then stops going to classes altogether, her parents have cause for concern.

The general rule in distinguishing between "normal" and "abnormal" is, if behavior interferes with a youngster's ability to function, then it may be considered abnormal or problematic.

In general, your teen shows normal behavior when he or she is able to function and perform well in everyday life, and is able to form and maintain relationships with family, friends, and others. The "normal" teen performs well in school, has friends, gets along with teachers, and feels happy and interested in life.

Measuring your child against the kid next door may be a natural tendency, but it's not a good idea. Circumstances and personalities vary so much from person to person, and adolescence brings on moment-to-moment changes within the same child. Therefore it helps to be familiar with the course of adolescent development and its most pressing issues.

Adolescence is like a trip through Alice's looking glass, where things don't appear as they are. Between the two ends of the normal adolescent spectrum there is a wide range of feelings and actions that constitute a teen's normal, sometimes predictable, or uncomfortable development. Teens stretch and test limits to develop.

Be careful to avoid labeling your child or his behavior. Even when said in a heated moment of anger, brands such as "crazy," "stupid," or "bad" can burn a painful impression on a youngster's mind and can have damaging effects on his self-esteem. Youngsters have a difficult enough time establishing identity and self-worth without being pigeonholed as a "poor student," "troublemaker," or "bad kid." They do respond to praise and positive rewards and reinforcements.

Since the time of Sigmund Freud, therapists have thought in terms of two major areas of life in which it is important to function well: love and work. Especially for teenagers, we believe it is important to add the area of play. Nearly every human activity fits into these three categories.

Teen Love

For your adolescent, love encompasses close personal relationships with family, peers, the opposite sex, and even him- or herself. At age twelve, an adolescent's experience of work and love is closer to that of a child's; at seventeen, it is closer to that of an adult. What's normal at one stage of adolescence may not be considered normal at another. An intense romance for a twelve-year-old may be premature. However, such a relationship is fairly normal for an eighteen-year-old.

Separation: When Your Child Becomes a Stranger

You may have the experience that your adolescent no longer seems to be the person you once knew. This can confuse your relationship, which may be becoming increasingly strained. Last month you were arguing with your sixteen-year-old about her desire to wear a black leather miniskirt to school; this morning she announced she was going on a weekend ski trip with "some friends" whom you haven't met.

Around age twelve kids begin to go through the process of breaking away from parents. This is often awkward and uncomfortable for everybody. Parents can feel the loss of the child, and the child loses the family as a reference point. Of course parents gain a teenager on his or her way to becoming an adult, and teens reap obvious rewards.

An early sign of this may be your child's wanting to get to school early to hang around the lockers with friends, rather than having breakfast with the family as usual. Being less interested in family activities and wanting to spend more time with friends is predictable and almost expected.

Even if you know what to expect, the first time your child

would rather just talk on the phone with friends than go to a movie with the family will no doubt hurt. Younger teens especially want to separate from their parents and feel grown up, but they feel guilty for hurting their parents and uneasy about the loss of security.

By age seventeen or eighteen these fears are usually worked through, and your youngster feels more comfortable being closer to the adult world. Separation from the family will not seem nearly as traumatic. A parent can have trouble letting go of an adolescent and may perceive this separation as an abnormality in the youngster. Here is a case of a normal progression:

> At twelve, Jessica loved Easter, and looked forward to going to church and singing in the choir. By age fifteen, she was trying to scare up transportation to get to Palm Springs with her girlfriends for spring break. And by age seventeen she just wanted to be alone with her boyfriend.

You may feel startled and uncomfortable when your generally cooperative, even-tempered teen becomes a downright surly, moody kid. Discomfort can turn to shock and concern when a fourteen-year-old's temper explodes and he tears the posters off his wall, and then says he doesn't know why. Chances are he cannot cope with his anger and frustration any better than you can. When he can't find another outlet for those feelings, they can bubble to the surface in a helpless, furious outburst. A lot of times youngsters themselves don't understand what's going on.

There may be confrontations at home, with a teen who always yells at one parent or won't talk to the other. What occurs depends largely on the dynamics of the family. But to some extent a child must reject his parents as a natural part of becoming a separate individual. This can be confusing for parents.

> The aunt, uncle, and cousins of fifteen-year-old Tanya were in town, and they came over for a meal. Rather than hugging everyone, chattering happily at the table, and playing with her cousins after dinner, as she used to, Tanya mumbled hello, stared at her plate during dinner, and then retreated to her room.

> Her parents felt angry, embarrassed, and confused. But such withdrawals are sometimes a normal part of a teenager's wide range of behavior.

Adolescents often reject the role they once played in the family and can be openly defiant. When defiance and rebellion rule the waters, sailing cannot be smooth.

It is normal for adolescents to assert their independence and distance themselves from the close relationships they had as children, including those with parents and siblings. Extremes are normal in adolescent development. Things may get uncomfortable—and at times maddening—for you and your teen. But it's the natural course of that process of growing up. You don't have to like or condone what is going on. You should attempt to listen, understand, and offer feedback.

An adolescent's search for and experience of love naturally shifts away from parents and siblings to peers, then often to a romantic involvement. It doesn't mean your child loves you any less; he's simply exploring his own range of potential relationships.

Conforming with Peers

Teenagers dress, talk, and act the way their friends do not only to fit in but also to rebel against laws parents have laid down. Even if you feel you're very lenient, chances are your youngster will feel smothered at times by family rules.

Boys are normally given independence earlier, although they are a little slower than girls in reaching puberty. They might start using slang and swearing early in adolescence, wanting to find a separate identity. All of these behaviors trumpet the message, "I'm not your little kid anymore. Don't treat me like a child!"

Sexuality

In the midst of the countless changes taking place in their bodies, it's natural for teenagers to examine their responses and reactions to their own sexuality. Sexual feelings are confusing, especially for younger adolescents who were just recently repulsed by the cootie-ridden opposite sex. Kids agonize over the etiquette of dating, how to be attractive, and how to respond to the stirring of sexual feelings.

It's probably difficult for you as a parent to think of your youngster moving toward adult sexuality. And you may not feel comfortable broaching the subject with him or her. Teens tend to gather some of the facts on their own; but parents should clarify confusion and answer questions. Girls often want to know if they're "feminine enough." Boys tend to question their masculinity.

A teen may experience some shyness over newly found interest in the opposite sex. Some experimentation can be expected. After all, your child, like it or not, is rushing headlong into adulthood, powered by hormones.

Any strong sexual drives can be a terrifying new sensation for your teenager. Your youngster may feel that someone—or something—else has taken control, especially if the opposite sex was regarded as "the enemy" for many years.

School dances and parties are normal ways for young adolescents to be together and to test the waters without having to be concerned about the pressures of dating yet. Your son may be attracted to a girl and simultaneously be terrified that she might actually want to go out with him. He may fear rejection. Such volleying doesn't do much for a youngster's confidence.

Insecurity and fears of inadequacy are part and parcel of the normal course of development for adolescents. Remember, however, that everyone develops at his or her own pace. You cannot automatically assume that your child will feel comfortable with what's happening to him just because he is old enough to drive.

A fairly safe rule of thumb is to be on the lookout for extremes. When an adolescent is either too sexually preoccupied or unable to interact with the opposite sex altogether, you may have some cause for concern, especially for your teen's sense of self-esteem.

Thirteen-year-old Christine started dressing very seductively, became sullen and withdrawn, and was seen getting into the car

> of a high school boy. Her parents' immediate reaction was to accuse her of being sexually active, saying things like, "Boys don't really like loose girls. They just use them."
>
> Christine's parents needed to look beyond the behavior to the motives to determine how Christine's self-esteem was tied to her attractiveness. Further insights revealed that Christine was doing poorly in school and felt her family was not supportive. So she was taken in by boys who told her she was pretty and gave her a sense of success and belonging.

For a thirteen-year-old, having sex is *not* usual behavior. But the seventeen-year-old boy and girl who struggle between the desire to have sex with each other and the wish to please their parents are experiencing a normal dilemma for that age.

However, the seventeen-year-old who shows no interest in peers or the opposite sex and watches television for hours on end might warrant some attention. When you are trying to draw the boundaries of what is normal, you must look closely at the age of the child concerned and the context.

Teens in their later years may begin dating and pairing off with boyfriends and girlfriends. This allows youngsters to try on the adult role of commitment to a mate, even if the "mate" changes frequently.

Remember that the transition from childhood to early adolescence is arduous. For many youngsters, it is a terrifying process that can scare them away from the opposite sex until well into adulthood. A boy's dancing with a girl for the first time or a girl's letting a boy kiss her is scary. You need to be encouraging of your child's social development. But the real power at this stage is the support of the peers. It's a lot easier to have the courage to start dating when your friends are doing it.

Some adolescents may question their sexuality or worry about fleeting attraction to same-sex friends to the point of wondering whether they are homosexual. This does *not* mean they are. It merely means that, because their sexuality is not yet well established, they are uncertain about what their roles are and about whether they are filling those roles. Passing thoughts like these do not necessarily mean that your child has homosexual tendencies.

It merely means that for the time being, sexuality is still a murky, ill-defined area.

If your teen is deeply troubled by thoughts such as these, however, you should definitely consider outside counsel to help work things through. One of the major functions of adolescence is to come to terms with identity. There are bound to be periods of doubt and uncertainty.

Teen Work

The second of the three aspects of adolescent life is work. Where work for an adult means the pursuit of a career, for an adolescent it means school. School is really the most significant part of a teenager's day. The number of hours and amount of effort that an adolescent puts into school are close to what an adult invests in a job. Your youngster's work is to master skills that will help him function in the adult world. School is a social and emotional, as well as academic, training ground. Beyond books and P.E. class, there are the issues of job performance, peer acceptance, and the formation of a social circle, as well as social rivalry and competition.

As your youngster becomes more and more attached to his or her peers and the "work" of school, your once congenial home environment may feel strained. Your teen may feel torn between wanting to please the family and wanting to please the peer group. There is likely to come a time when your teen simply does not seem to find a comfortable way to fit into the family anymore, especially when family standards don't match those of the peer group. And while the cloak of family warmth once felt cozy and snug, it now can feel too tight. Besides, the peer group is a lot more stylish.

As your adolescent shifts her sense of identity from the family to her peer group, she may not want to wear the patent leather shoes you think she looks so cute in but the high-top sneakers all her friends are wearing.

To a young adolescent it's of monumental importance to have the right stuff: clothes, music, even vocabulary. Girls especially will break off into cliques to fortify their social identity. Young girls often talk a long time on the phone with friends or chat endlessly about boys or the latest rock star. But they are still more or less under the control of their parents. By sixteen they generally have far more independence.

A young adolescent may frequently talk about what went on at school and is likely to want his parents to attend parents' night and the school play. Younger teens want to do well to please their parents and will often share their problems and concerns with parents. So it's easier to keep track of how they're doing emotionally, as well as academically.

As teens get older they are more apt to want to share problems with peers. By the time they are ready to graduate from high school, they still want their parents to be proud, but they are pursuing interests that are of more value to themselves. They show this by selecting their own courses in high school, and possibly a college and major. They may ask for input from their parents, but they ultimately want to feel they have made their own decisions. Teens like to be autonomous, which they become by earning some of their own money and structuring their own time. They can't be forced to want more responsibility; they usually want to arrive at it themselves, like Mary and Daniel.

> According to her parents, Mary seemed to blossom in her senior year of high school. She took more initiative to finish her homework and took charge of filing her college applications. Previously she was always running out of money, but recently she took a part-time job as a department store clerk.

> Daniel developed a strong interest in skiing when he was fifteen, and though he lived across the country, he dreamed of taking a ski trip to Colorado. At the end of his sophomore year, he got a job as a dishwasher in order to save money for a ski trip his junior year.

Participating in extracurricular activities helps define a teen's personality. A young adolescent may be willing to explore piano or dance lessons because a parent thinks it's a good idea. Later, a teen should have developed strong interests of his or her own—such as playing guitar in a rock band, going out for sports, planning a bicycle trip with friends, or becoming involved in local politics.

Your teen may stop taking your advice or seeming to value your opinion; it's normal that this turning away will sting for both you and your child. When "Daddy's little girl" becomes her father's biggest worry, try to keep in mind that separating from you is at least as much of a conflict for your teen – but youngsters often lack the verbal skills to express that.

When this anticipated break starts to occur, let your knowledge of adolescence guide you. Remembering that it is uncommon for a seventeen-year-old to be preoccupied with her parents' approval may help ease the pain. And when adolescence is behind you, it's likely that you will reconnect with your adult child in a new, and in some ways better, relationship.

Let's take a look at what a child's performance in school might say about what's going on inside of him or her. School functioning can be an indicator of how a child is feeling about him- or herself. A child who is doing fairly well academically and is active in sports or extracurricular activities may be feeling pretty content. A teen who is failing miserably, even though he has tested as being bright, may be having trouble not with mastering the subject but with perfecting other skills, such as fitting in with peers or feeling comfortable dating.

He might, for instance, be feeling conflict between being accepted by one significant group – his peers – and rejecting another very important group – his parents. Your son may feel conflict over attending his high school's football game, where a female classmate has asked to meet him; his younger sister's class play is on the same night, however, and the whole family plans to attend together.

If your teen has always earned high grades in school, you might assume that trend would continue. But when you consider all the radical changes taking place during puberty, there is no cause for alarm if your youngster's grades dip a bit now and then. It is not acceptable, however, for the drop in grades to slide into regular failing marks. And a good student who drops or gets kicked out of school may need help.

Extremes go both ways. It may be a relief to have a teenager who doesn't go out with a "wild crowd," but you might be equally concerned if your youngster clings anxiously and doesn't begin to take an interest in and identify with peers. It may be of serious concern if your teenager stays alone in his or her bedroom all day long and never socializes with family or friends; being overly helpful at home can also be cause for concern.

> Susan, sixteen, is her single mother's right-hand helper. She fixes dinner for her three brothers every night and is eager to earn extra money to help with the bills. Her mother is grateful for her help, but is also concerned that her daughter is not spending enough time socializing with friends her own age.

Peer Pressure, Drugs, and Alcohol

Curiosity and some experimentation and exploration may be along the normal path. Drugs and alcohol become more accessible to teens as they get older and start going to parties. There will be peer pressure to try these new experiences.

So although you'd rather he didn't, your teen will probably let liquor touch his lips before he reaches adulthood. What is not normal is any abuse of alcohol or other substances. This does not mean we condone drug or alcohol use, nor that you should. Or that at any age drug or alcohol abuse is acceptable. It's simply true that many adolescents do experiment with the "adult" experience of drinking and smoking.

When Work and Love Go Wrong

Although you may think your teen can't know the meaning of the word, teens experience stress in many forms. It comes at them from school, peer pressure, independence from the family, and issues of sexuality, to name a few sources. In early adolescence, stress is complicated by biological changes. Later, the final stages of finding individual identity play more of a role, in senior year of high school, for instance.

> Nancy, a high school senior, has final exams in a week, and college applications are due. She is staying up until midnight every night worrying about whether she's going to pass with high

enough grades to get into her first-choice college and keep from disappointing her parents.

Every adolescent has to endure a certain amount of mild anxiety and depression. An adolescent is going from having the relatively protected identity of a child into the complete unknown.

Learning how to become an adult is not like learning how to ride a bicycle: you don't just magically "catch on" after a few skinned knees and sail merrily on your way. And there's no such thing as training wheels. There is no sense of immediate accomplishment. The tasks facing an adolescent are not that easy; in fact, they take years to master.

Play Works in a Teen's Favor

For adolescents a third area, play, should be added to the centrally important love and work. A teen cannot play as he did as a child, nor can he play like an adult. Consider that stress is a large part of adolescence. So the ability to have fun and not take all that's happening too seriously is especially important.

Play is related to your teen's ability to enjoy leisure activity, put aside the stresses and problems of life, and become immersed in pleasurable, fun pursuits. When you understand that most adolescents act and react to stress the way they do because they feel unsettled and in a state of flux, you may feel more accepting toward changes. By keeping an open mind, you can actually reduce the stress that both you and your teen experience.

What's Your Parenting Style?

We find three common parenting styles, or ways in which parents relate to their adolescents. Knowing your style can help you better understand your teen.

1. *The indulgent parents.* These parents rarely discipline their youngster. They may be quite permissive and feel they have less control over their teen. They may allow their youngster to break

minor social rules or laws, such as driving before acquiring a license, or drinking.

2. *The-rules-are-rules parents.* These parents are often strict, and enforce rules using rewards and strong discipline. They may themselves have come from backgrounds in which everything had to be in place, and rigid rules governed the household. These parents frequently have jobs in which they are expected to follow orders.

3. *The middle-ground parents.* This is the most common parenting style. These parents can be strict in setting and enforcing rules but permissive in other instances. They believe their youngster has rights but that their authority rules. These parents usually manage to maintain a good mix of tough and tender, of limit-setting and nurturing. Their teen does not always like them, and there are painful and difficult times. But family members respect each other, and harmony is more easily achieved.

Doing What You Can to Better Relations

As hard as it is to understand your child's conflicting feelings during this period, your empathy and compassion are essential. You can delight in his or her many accomplishments. Your youngster's internal struggle between body and emotion may temporarily make him or her miserable to live with. He's not misbehaving or challenging your authority when he says he "hates" you or is ungrateful. It is simply a teen's biological and societal task to find an identity separate from you. And this means pushing away.

What will help you maintain a better relationship with your teen is to understand that this is a time in the life cycle when a person must struggle with major issues of identity. Try to focus on your youngster's strengths and accomplishments.

The struggle is not your teen's alone. You too will have to deal with the inconsistencies of your budding adult—who one moment masters the foe of geometry and the next is convinced that acne is terminal. Here is a typical case:

> Fourteen-year-old Marie doesn't understand why she can't stay out at the arcade as late as her friends. She feels her parents mistrust her, though she has not given them reason. They insist

they want to help her stay out of trouble. She throws tantrums and shuts down the lines of communication because her parents' lack of trust assaults her self-esteem.

Lending Your Teen a Hand

Although you and your teen may clash over her wishes that you find frivolous or inappropriate, you *can* help matters along by giving an inch when appropriate. Here is a typical scenario between parent and teen.

Your sophomore in high school wants to buy chartreuse stretch pants and a pretorn, oversized sweatshirt to fit in with what her friends are wearing. Which response would you make?

A. Point out that fads change every season, and it's ridiculous to spend good money on something she'll only wear a few times.

B. Tell her that if she really wanted to make a statement, she would set her own style and not follow her classmates' tastes like a sheep.

C. Acknowledge in word and deed that your teen's desire to fit in is understandable. While you can't afford every passing fad, you would like to help her assess what's important to her and figure out how to obtain it.

If you see yourself as parent A or B, you may be missing your teen's message, which is "I need to belong." If you chose C, you have learned that an ounce of cooperation will help you get along with your teen without sacrificing your authority—and will allow you to reserve a pound of parental energy for when you really need it. In this case you are willing to listen while setting limits.

This response allows you to treat your teen like a fair-minded, rational adult, and to allow her to accept responsibility for what she wants. Besides keeping the peace and showing a willingness to compromise, this response will support harmless activities that promote your teen's sense of belonging.

Remember that during this volatile period of adolescence, there are forces at work that neither you nor your teen understand. If he or she is in turmoil, your teen may not be able to tell you what's going on. But you can learn what danger signs might indicate that problems are more serious than "just a phase."

Once you are familiar with what is considered "normal" behavior, you will be better equipped to spot abnormal behavior. When the floundering and uncertainty of the teenage years interfere with your teen's ability to function normally, you know it's time to get your youngster some help.

3

Crossing the Line: When Do You Call in the Reinforcements?

> Your daughter's crushing depression over not making the swim team lingers on for more than a month.
>
> Your son loses interest in eating dinner with the family, going to movies with friends, or playing in the band. He stays in his room all the time listening to one song over and over. His grades have declined, and his personal hygiene has become deplorable. He has turned into a complete loner.
>
> Your daughter complains of headaches, stomach problems, fatigue, and other stress-related ailments with no medical origin. She's often irritable and frustrated. Within the last several months she has begun to eat compulsively.
>
> Your son sneaks out to drink and get high with his friends, and frequently comes home drunk.
>
> Your daughter begins to put things in order and starts apologizing for things she's done to hurt you. She's begun talking about death as a type of fulfillment.

As the parent of an adolescent you may be wondering,

> "Where is the line between normal and abnormal behavior?"
>
> "What warning signs point to a teen in trouble?"

"How many of my teen's conflicts should I realistically try to handle alone?"

"How would I recognize signs that my youngster needs the attention of a professional therapist?"

You're determined to notice any flashing lights that might signal your teen's in danger. But on another level you may not *want* to admit there could be something seriously troubling your youngster. Perhaps his or her odd behavior has become so routine that you don't perceive it as worrisome. Or it could be that tension, hostility, and even rage have grown between you, obscuring signs that your teen is in pain.

Professional psychotherapy can provide the light at the end of the tunnel. But first you need to learn to recognize the darker side of teenage behavior. For every shade in the spectrum of "normal" adolescent behavior, there is one hue slightly less bright. By learning to distinguish between one of your teen's blue moods and a black clinical depression, you can get help for him or her when it's needed.

When Do Depression and Anxiety Become Serious Problems?

Every adolescent has to endure a certain amount of mild anxiety and depression. It is when these "moods" become incapacitating—and interfere with normal work, love, or play—that your child may need help. Learn to distinguish between your teen's sad moods and what is known as serious or *clinical* depression—which is severe enough to warrant immediate professional attention.

Depression

Clinical depression can lead to dysfunction in a youngster, such as not having friends, not getting along with kids at school or home, causing chaos in the family, exhibiting self-destructive, aggressive, or violent behavior, and possibly attempting suicide.

We use the word *depression* in our everyday lives to describe when we're feeling sad or blue. Depression exists on a continuum of mild, moderate, and extreme. Here is a case of relatively mild depression:

> When seventeen-year-old Julie got a low score on her math SAT exam, she felt low all afternoon, and told her mother that she was too upset to eat dinner.

Clinical depression is more intense and/or can linger on, causing profound emotional problems or even suicidal thoughts:

> Liz, a girl in the same class who was trying to win an engineering scholarship to college, also scored very low on the math SAT test. After three weeks of feeling consumed by her depression and worry, she had convinced herself that she was a complete failure. She went to the medicine cabinet and took half a bottle of her mother's mild sleeping pills.

What defines clinical depression are intensity and duration—how deep the depression is and how long it lasts. It may also be defined by specific clusters of symptoms, such as a sad mood, alterations in appetite, sleep disturbance, thoughts of death, and feelings of hopelessness.

In the case just described, performing well on the math exam was so central to Liz's sense of self-worth that by failing to get the score she needed to win the scholarship, she felt a deep sense of depression and loss. She believed her life might as well be over. Her depression was precipitated—not caused—by the event of performing poorly on the test.

Spotting clinical depression can be a tough call. Parents of a teen who attempts suicide may say they never realized their son had been depressed. Another teen might sulk, become a loner, and show more obvious signs of depression:

> Sixteen-year-old David has been suspended several times for truancy, fighting, and being disrespectful to his teachers. He was recently suspended for throwing a book across the room when asked to leave the class. When asked why, he shrugged his shoulders and said he didn't know.

David stays in his room playing his drums, watches television, and drinks whiskey to help him fall asleep. He has no respect or feelings for himself or anyone around him, or so he says.

Sixteen-year-old Kim has moved out of her family home and is living with an eighteen-year-old girlfriend. Her room there is in total disarray. She refuses to let her parents come over and is too depressed to go to school. She demands that her parents hire a private tutor to teach her in her own bedroom. Her parents cannot get her to explain what's wrong.

Kim is unable to tell her parents about a sexual assault that occurred a year before on her way home from school. Her relationship with her parents, she feels, was so strained before the incident that she fears they would blame her. Kim feels trapped. She spends much of the day attempting to talk on the phone with various girlfriends, all of whom rebuff her for her antisocial behavior.

Her parents attempt to be very "progressive," but they don't know how to approach her. They are afraid that their daughter may try to kill herself.

Thoughts of suicide or an actual suicide attempt should be taken very seriously and intervention obtained immediately. Although teens may sometimes wonder if anyone would miss them if they were gone, *never* assume your child is just making idle threats or manipulating to get your attention!

If a teen does not know who he is and why he is here, he may question the reasons for and the value of his existence. Most teens wonder about their purpose in life, but a child who sees no reason for his being on this earth, and attempts to harm himself, needs immediate professional attention.

Anxiety

Anxiety, simply put, is fear. In the case of anxiety, a person cannot identify exactly of what he is afraid. When a person is functioning normally, fear can work in his or her favor. For instance, if you're walking down a dark alley in a bad neighborhood, feeling fearful and anxious is a useful protection mechanism. But when fear becomes incapacitating, or occurs without cause, it can be paralyzing, as it is for Steve.

> Fourteen-year-old Steve frets constantly about his grades and whether he will live up to the standards of his father, a circuit court judge. He feels he must excel at everything he attempts, including sports and dating. His worries become obsessions. Although his obsessions are psychological, they manifest themselves physically. He becomes more anxious, talks rapidly, and doesn't respond to things said to him. He feels strong internal pressure to succeed in school and socially.
>
> Steve's worries expand to the point where he can no longer function. He forgets to eat or shower, cannot sleep or be cheered up, and needs constant reassurance from others.

Anxiety is a physiological response closely related to fear. Professional help may be required when someone is anxious about or fearful of ordinary things that don't faze most people, such as going to school.

> Fifteen-year-old Patti had such anxiety about going to school that she vomited on the classroom floor on the first day. She was so humiliated that she could not go back. Each morning, she would leave home as if to go to school, but instead she would walk around the park or go window shopping. Her mother believed she was in school; but Patti was too terrified to return. Her anxiety was incapacitating.

Anxiety may be brought on by a humiliating experience, as in Patti's case. An anxious teen may be more shy than his aggressive classmates. Or he may be paralyzed by a fear of failing. A youngster may feel such high expectations to succeed that anything he does is bound to fall short.

When Kids Don't Say No to Drugs or Alcohol

Sometimes a teen may turn to drugs and alcohol to quell anxiety or alleviate depression. This can be an attempt to self-medicate emotional pain. But substance abuse is typically a symptom of a deeper problem. Low self-esteem might be the real disease. If your daughter doesn't like herself or feels anxious or depressed—about not getting asked out on a date, or a heartbreakingly severe case of acne—she may smoke a joint or drink several beers to numb the pain. A youngster who doesn't function in love, work, and play, who, for example, cannot go to school because he is too depressed, may use drugs or alcohol. Depression is a factor in many cases of substance abuse.

Anxiety may also show up in an eating disorder or substance abuse. A teen may feel so anxious that she smokes pot to "calm her down" or use food as a substitute for self-love.

If your child is using drugs or alcohol to self-medicate, it is an abnormal response to the pressures of adolescent life. The paradox that arises is that using drugs or alcohol may cause your youngster to feel even more worthless, which can lead to self-destructive feelings and behavior, even suicide.

Addiction to alcohol or any other drug is serious and warrants professional help. Beyond being a health hazard, it will affect how your child functions in school, and with family and peer groups, and will squelch his own development. In the appendix we list resources to turn to if you suspect that your teen is dependent on drugs or alcohol. The first step is to take it very seriously.

Some research shows that alcoholism can run in a family. If either parent has a drug or drinking problem, your child may be more prone to dependency, and you should keep an eye on him or her. Addiction to alcohol or drugs may intensify or precipitate depression, or increase a teen's tendency toward suicide.

Adolescents often feel inadequate and fear rejection. When a teen believes he is not good enough or is not well-liked, he may start hanging out with a crowd of kids who are using drugs, who generally make fewer demands on him than normally functioning kids. At this point he may start using drugs. His drug addict friends are always willing to party. Drugs become the whole point of getting together. The group activity becomes the pursuit of the drug and the use of it. The pressure to interact is off.

Though psychotherapy may be an essential part of the treatment plan for an addicted adolescent, it is often not enough. It may be necessary to become involved in a twelve-step recovery program, intensive outpatient or inpatient treatment, and family involvement, or a combination thereof.

If alcohol or drugs are interfering in your youngster's areas of love, social relationships, school, or play, consider taking the first step toward getting a professional assessment and help.

Sexuality

Awakening sexuality is a major and essential component of adolescence. It's also an aspect of growing up that tends to worry parents a lot as these cases show.

> Fourteen-year-old Will ran away from home to escape his abusive stepfather. Living hand-to-mouth, he became involved with a ring of male prostitutes. He lived on the street and started abusing alcohol. Will's sexual development started too early and then verged into self-destructive behavior. He may never have a chance to form healthy relationships.

> Fifteen-year-old Donna is beautiful, tall, and physically mature for her age. She is flattered by the attention of a high school senior, who convinces her to have sex with him on their first date. When she becomes pregnant after secretly dating him for a few months, Donna is shocked when the father of her child expresses his intent to attend college in another state. After concealing her pregnancy for three months, she is forced to tell her parents. She drops out of school to have her baby, determined she will raise it herself.

> Seventeen-year-old Robin has been sexually active for a year. She takes birth control pills to avoid getting pregnant but does not protect herself further. During a summer vacation at the beach, she has a number of flings with young men about whom she knows nothing. A year later she is diagnosed as carrying the AIDS virus.

In the "old days" sexual promiscuity—or mere experimentation—meant risking one's reputation, unwanted pregnancy, and perhaps venereal disease. In today's increasingly complicated world, it can be deadly. You may or may not accept that your adolescent could be sexually active, but please be sure he or she knows the facts about AIDS. Call your local health department for information to pass along.

Is Your Child Under Stress?

It may seem ludicrous to think of your teen being under stress. After all, he has all his needs met, doesn't have to support a family, and should be essentially worry-free. But the fact is that teens do experience stress. In fact stress can be a major factor in a youngster's behavior.

For adolescents "acting out" is a barometer of what's actually going on in their heads. They may engage in socially unacceptable behaviors that range from shoplifting or fighting to excessive sexual experimentation. Most often, this sort of self-destructive behavior indicates a lot of internal anger and turmoil. It is serious, beyond the realm of normal adolescent development, and needs to be treated as such.

No matter how good a job you do as a parent, there are circumstances beyond your control that may influence your teen and lead him or her astray. Be aware of situations in which your child may need additional help to cope with problems.

The intensity, quality, and number of stresses have a lot to do with whether they cause a teen the kind of problems that need treatment. If a seventeen-year-old's girlfriend dies in a car accident, the resulting stress is more likely to need attention than not making the basketball playoffs. Adolescence is a stress in itself. When too many more factors are added, a youngster's system can get overwhelmed.

> Fifteen-year-old Greg is volatile and emotional. When he gets cut from the basketball team and his girlfriend breaks up with him, he seems to snap; he runs four red lights on the way home from school and crashes into a tree. People get scared of him. He becomes routinely violent. When he threatens the assistant coach with a knife, the school principal calls the police.

Uncontrollable temper or rage in young males can signal depression, which can cause teens to turn anger against others—

or themselves. Anger seems to go either inward or against the world. Deep down, teens sometimes turn anger against the world rather than having to feel deep anger against themselves.

Many teens experience profound self-loathing. They are neither children nor adults. They have not mastered the necessary skills of adulthood, although they may be asked to assume many of the responsibilities—even to the point of bringing in part of the family income. Such a teen may feel all alone or that no one is interested in taking care of him. This often occurs in teens when one or both parents have a drug problem, as in Lisa's case.

> The father of fourteen-year-old Lisa is a successful businessman. He has had many affairs with women half his age. Although her parents are still married, Lisa feels extreme stress because of discord between them. Her dad is addicted to cocaine and has used it in front of her. He unsuccessfully concealed his long-term affair with his secretary. Lisa knows things are wrong.

> The older brother of thirteen-year-old Phil drowned last year. Although he had nothing to do with the accident, Phil takes some responsibility for his brother's death. He believes his parents would have preferred that he had died instead.

General Behavior Problems

Many teens experience not just a single identifiable problem area but a combination of several. A teen may drink heavily, shoplift occasionally, and disobey his parents. The problems are serious, as these cases demonstrate:

> Sixteen-year-old Nick starts ditching school and spends several mornings a week getting high with his friends. It gets to the point where he has missed so much school that he can't catch up. He decides he might as well cut out for the rest of the term. He gets expelled for smoking pot at school, and because he has no job he hangs out with his other friends who cut class.

> Fifteen-year-old Anna has been babysitting for her next-door neighbors for three years. It is discovered that she has been

drinking hard liquor from their liquor cabinet and replacing what she drinks with water.

She carries a thermos of vodka to school with her and takes swigs at her locker between classes. Her P.E. teacher becomes concerned when Anna falls down a flight of stairs and breaks her arm—and begins to laugh.

The school nurse is alarmed to discover that Anna is drunk. Until this time, Anna's parents had no idea she had a drinking problem.

Seventeen-year-old Tina is with a crowd of people who are partying. She is drinking her fifth beer when one of her friends suggests going downtown to buy some crack. Tina reluctantly goes along for the ride, not wanting to appear afraid.

They wind up at a spot well known for availability of drugs. Tina and another girl wait in the car. The kids buying the drugs are arrested by two under-cover cops. Tina and the other passenger are also arrested.

Needless to say, if your teen becomes involved in crime—such as shoplifting, drug peddling, and violence—it indicates that he or she needs help. Once you determine that your teen's behavior has indeed crossed the line between normal and abnormal, it's time to call in the reinforcements.

4

Addressing Teens with Special Needs

Adoption, Divorce, and Death

Is your youngster adopted?

Has your family experienced a divorce?

Has your teen experienced the death of a relative or close friend?

Loss is a significant psychological issue that directly relates to a teen's self-esteem. The effects of special circumstances such as being adopted, parents' divorce, or the death of a parent or sibling, need to be examined. While being adopted by a loving family—and even the breakup of a bad marriage—can be positive overall, they add a dimension and often stress to a teen. To deal with complex issues, a teen may benefit from talking to someone outside the family.

Adoption

Although many adoptive families function as a happy, loving, and supportive unit, it has been well noted in the literature on adolescence that adoptees frequently have a particularly stressful time during this development stage. This is true for a number of reasons. An adolescent's search for identity is complicated by the fact that an adopted child has special questions about his or her identity. For many adopted adolescents, this question leaves a lingering feeling that their birth parents did not love them enough to keep them.

For an adopted youngster, the adolescent years can seem to be much less safe in terms of dealing with and confronting the issue of adoption than are the childhood years. There are many more issues that lead the teenage adopted child to question his or her adoption.

This is further compounded by the fact that adoptees sometimes feel "different" or "inadequate." This may cause feelings of anger and depression, and may result in behavior problems, as in this case:

> Michael is a fourteen-year-old adopted boy who has become aggressive toward his eleven-year-old brother, the natural child of their parents. Not only does Michael tease his younger brother, but at times strikes him, berates him, and destroys his possessions.
>
> The boys' parents had always thought that some sibling rivalry was normal, but they become concerned when Michael exhibits a self-righteous attitude and no sense of remorse.

For the adopted child, pulling away from parents presents an added fear that each step toward independence and adulthood is a step away from the love of the adoptive parents, accompanied perhaps by guilt, regret, and insecurity. Even in the safest, most stable, and loving environment, an adopted teen may experience additional anguish over growing up.

How parents address the issues surrounding adoption with their teen largely influences the teen's self-perception. Some adoptive parents coddle their teen, failing to set the limits, enforce rules, or make demands—all steps necessary to the teen's healthy development.

Parents often fear their adopted teen will feel rejected, so they set few limits. This often backfires when the teen perceives that he or she is "different," or not worthy of the proper guidance that peers or siblings receive.

Parents may fear their child will not love them unless they are indulgent and lenient. In the absence of fair and firm boundaries, however, a teen often experiences more turmoil and stress than he or she would otherwise, as Kurt did.

> Kurt's parents had never disciplined their son, fearing he would love them less, or feel alienated and unloved. By age sixteen, Kurt had become unruly and destructive, and used alcohol and marijuana. He began to stay out hours after his ten o'clock curfew and felt school was not important.

The internal stress of adopted children is compounded by the reactions of their adoptive parents, siblings, and the absent birth parents.

The issue of adoption carries with it some very serious implications in terms of the development of a teen's self-concept and self-esteem. Other family traumas, such as the death of a sibling, may in some ways exaggerate the feelings that a youngster has about being adopted, which are always there unless they are addressed by the parents.

> Linda was twelve when her five-year-old sister, a natural child, died of leukemia. The family was devastated. Because she had always felt somewhat guilty about having been given up by her natural mother, Linda somehow assumed a degree of responsibility for her sister's death. Perceiving that the family would have preferred that *she* die, Linda ran away.

As adolescents struggle with issues of independence and responsibility, they often perceive that their parents push them too hard or ignore them. For the adopted child, this tendency may be exacerbated. Kids often learn to "push their parents' buttons" by using their adoption as kind of a weapon. An adopted teen who has his driving privileges revoked for getting too many speeding tickets may accuse his parents of not loving him or of punishing him for being adopted.

As a teen, an adopted child may fear being pushed out of the nest before he or she is ready. The special pressures of adopted teens may result in behavior or emotional problems that can be addressed in therapy. The deep, underlying personal conflicts of a teen can often be exaggerated by adoption.

In therapy there may be hidden or disguised feelings that the teen has harbored perhaps for most of his or her life which need to be addressed and worked through. A therapist can facilitate the gaining of some insight into a teen's feelings and behavior, and help him or her connect the feelings and issues about being adopted to the problems. It is not at all unusual for adopted adolescents to need individual therapy to unearth, explore, and attempt to resolve the family dynamic issues that may be associated with adoption.

How the Parents' Divorce Can Affect an Adolescent

The issue of identity is essential to understanding how divorce can affect a teen. The struggle for self-identity is compounded by the threat divorce poses to the family identity. One component of a teen's self-concept is a part of the family unit. When that unit unravels, the youngster's self-image often frays as well.

Regardless of the reasons, a teen may blame himself for his parents' breakup, especially if he has caused problems within the family. A youngster may act out in an attempt to keep the parents together. Teens may feel that if only they had been "better" children their parents would not be divorcing. Even in the midst of their own turmoil, it is essential for divorcing parents to determine how their teen perceives him- or herself as part of the breaking-down process.

Some teens may blame one parent exclusively, reject him or her, and lose whatever role model benefits that parent might provide.

When a teen's parents are not getting along, their fights, divorce proceedings, custody battle, and perceived change of identity cause the youngster incredible stress, which can result in a multitude of emotional and behavioral problems.

No matter how smooth the divorce becomes, or how much the action actually improves the lives of all concerned, a teen will always feel a sense of loss and abandonment. The household is disrupted, someone has to move, and that often includes the teen.

A family's financial situation also changes, which can feel less secure to the teen. Some teens show obvious signs of stress:

> Tom was fifteen when his father announced that he and Tom's mother were divorcing. The boy felt an intense rage and anger, and a fear this his life would be destroyed. Tom stormed out of the house and spent the next two days at the home of a friend, without letting his parents know where he was.

Positive parent interaction and a loving, nurturing family life can foster the development of a healthy and positive sense of self-esteem in an adolescent. So when a family is in crisis, that support system begins to break down.

Death of a Parent

Perhaps the greatest trauma a teen can experience is the death of a parent. Although it is in some ways similar to divorce, death is far more devastating to a youngster. It is often helpful to work through the grief process with a professional, even if the teen seems to be coping well, since that professional can offer the perspective of a caring outsider.

> Phoebe's mother died of breast cancer when Phoebe was thirteen, and she went into a prolonged period of grief and withdrawal. Angry toward her friends for having mothers and at the world for allowing her tragedy, Phoebe was afraid to get close to her father, in case he also died.

In therapy, Phoebe slowly expressed her deep grief, feelings of abandonment, and longing for her mother. She was afraid that loving another person would only lead to further loss and abandonment. Phoebe's loss was so personal—so deep and painful to discuss—that initially she needed to explore those feelings in the context of a relationship with a caring adult who was outside the family. As time passed, Phoebe found some solace in being in a group with other adolescents who had lost a parent. Therapy gave her a place to explore these complex, sometimes contradictory feelings of loss and sadness, anger and fear of abandonment, and the desire to hide her need to be loved.

The teen who shows no emotional expression of mourning may be in great distress internally, and may be attempting to be strong for the benefit of other family members.

> David, age sixteen, came home from school one day and learned that his father had died in an accident. Though he and his father had been very close, David showed little sign of emotion over the loss.
>
> He became withdrawn, and after the funeral, during which he did not cry, he said to his mother, "I guess this makes me the man of the house." Over the next six months he showed little evidence of grieving but became more and more angry toward those around him.

Sometimes when the parent of an adolescent dies, that child is in the midst of rebelling against that parent. Kids may feel that their rebellion was so terrible that it killed the parent. These intense feelings of guilt and responsibility must be dealt with and are often most successfully worked through in therapy or grief counseling.

5

Exploring the Range of Therapy Choices

In what type of therapy should my teen be involved?

Do different therapists approach problems differently?

Which approach might be best for my youngster?

Once you have determined that your adolescent would benefit from professional therapy, it's a good idea to familiarize yourself with the options available to you.

Because the needs, senses of reality, actions, and reactions of teens often contrast so much with those of adults, their unique problems need to be addressed in an equally sensitive and unique manner. Just as pediatric medicine differs from adult medicine, therapy for adolescents is specially geared to address the issues of that age group. And some therapists are better trained and experienced in working with adolescents than others.

There are different approaches to therapy, as well as different settings in which to experience it. Being aware of all your options and knowing the benefits and drawbacks of each can help you make more intelligent, informed choices for your teen, and can restore your sense of control over the situation.

Adolescents who are experiencing conflict or difficulty in some aspect of their lives are usually not motivated to seek therapy on their own. They tend to be directed toward professional help by a parent, school authority, family practitioner, or church counselor.

Sometimes a youngster has been "threatened" with having to see a therapist because of behavior problems, like being suspended from school. Because therapy is not usually a teen's idea, he or she can lack motivation or be resistant to the notion and the process. Initially, teens view therapy as a form of punishment or as "another adult trying to tell them what to do."

It is almost inevitable that when first in therapy, an adolescent will be suspicious that the therapist is allied with the parents and is thus "the enemy." But through the careful guidance of a therapist and the consistent love and support of family, a teen should eventually learn to trust adults, as well as him- or herself.

Building Trust

Remember the sixties battle cry "Don't trust anyone over thirty"? Tailored to adolescence, that motto might read "Don't trust anyone over twenty-one." Often, kids are simply wary of the motives of adults—especially when the youngsters and adults are in crisis with each other, as teens often are with parents, teachers, and other adult authority figures. Especially in the beginning, therapy may seem like a tug-of-war. Trust is the first issue that needs to be addressed within the therapeutic process.

Just as youngsters test limits their parents set, adolescents may show up late for therapy, miss a session, or call for extra appointments to test the therapist. Don't take it as a signal that therapy isn't working or should be discontinued. It's all a part of a natural process to see who's in control.

Parents and teens are frequently interested in using the therapeutic process for different agendas. Parents might want their teen to work out school behavior problems, whereas a teenager may be more concerned about problems in his or her romantic relationship. It requires a skilled therapist to give the youngster the sense that his or her issues are relevant and vital, while not ignoring the issues the parents view as pressing.

Parents must understand that therapy will not get very far unless there is a confidential relationship between the therapist and the adolescent. Legally, the privileged communication exists between the parents and the therapist. Since it's essential that the teen trust the therapist, parents must almost always voluntarily respect the confidentiality between the youngster and the therapist if therapy is to progress, as this case demonstrates:

> Sixteen-year-old Josh is brought to a therapist because he was suspended from school for fighting. Initially, he views therapy as a punishment, and expects the therapist to continue the lecture his father and the principal started. He is therefore less than trusting and receptive.
>
> When the therapist starts talking about Josh's interest in cars, the boy begins to relax and open up a little.

Josh's parents need to have selected a therapist carefully enough to trust that he knows what he is doing, and that this process will be helpful in the long run. Only after establishing a trusting relationship with the patient can the therapist do his work.

Individual Psychotherapy

For the most part, when parents seek therapy for their adolescent, they turn to individual therapy—that which focuses more on the teen. In individual psychotherapy, the therapist meets in session with the adolescent for the full forty-five to fifty minutes. The youngster may provide his or her own transportation to the session and may be in charge of keeping and maintaining the appointment hour.

Individual therapy seems to be indicated when the problems the adolescent faces are needing a specific focus on the individual. This offers the advantage of giving the adolescent a relationship with an adult which is free of parental requirements of socializing and discipline. In time, it allows for a deep and ongoing feeling of companionship. It is hoped that a teen will carry that feeling of trust with him or her beyond therapy and adolescence into adulthood.

A therapist seeing an adolescent in individual therapy may meet with one or both parents periodically throughout the course of treatment.

The primary approaches used in individual therapy currently include psychodynamic therapy, behavior therapy, humanistic therapy, and eclectic therapy.

Different therapists have different orientations that may in some way influence how they act with and react to your teen and family. How you relate to a specific therapist and how he or she formulates problems and solutions with your teen and the family is partly determined by the setting (individual, family, or group therapy), as well as by the particular therapist's theoretical orientation and personality.

When you walk into a therapist's office to interview him or her, what's most important is that you and your teen feel a sense of connection with that therapist. You will care about how the therapist understands problems and approaches solutions. So understanding theoretical orientations will give you more of the information you need to make the best decision for your adolescent. Let's take a look at how different therapists might approach the case of Mike.

> The parents of fourteen-year-old Mike were divorced a year ago. Since then Mike has divided his time between home, where he lives with his mother and two younger sisters, and the home of his father, who has remarried and is living across town with his new wife.
>
> Mike's grades have fallen. He is often angry, sullen and disrespectful. He doesn't respond to his mother's attempts to discipline him. His father, who wants to get on with his new life, is a rather brutal disciplinarian.
>
> Because he has been told to "act like a man," Mike feels he can't show his hurt. He expresses it through emotional outbursts of rage directed toward his younger sisters. More vulnerable and willing to show their emotions, the girls seem weak to Mike and are an easy target for his hostility.
>
> Mike's mother is concerned that his father is becoming too harsh with their son, though she feels she cannot handle the child's discipline. Together they agree their son needs to see a therapist.

According to his or her orientation, a therapist might address Mike's situation in different ways:

A psychodynamic therapist might explore with Mike his anger toward his parents for breaking up the family and leaving him without a father. Through talking with this therapist, Mike might discover that he is angry at his mother for not trying harder to make her marriage work or to keep her husband at home. Mike might also express anger at his father for abandoning and rejecting the family, and for starting a new one.

A psychodynamic therapist might explore earlier experiences in the family that contribute to Mike's current outbursts. He or she may talk with Mike about his need for a father figure.

If problems are long-standing or involve major trauma early in life, and particularly if a teen is dealing with the loss of a parent or loved one, psychodynamic therapy might be the most effective approach. The focus of the psychodynamic approach in therapy is to help the teen understand how earlier developmental issues may be affecting present ones.

Common affected areas include sexuality, aggression, and the teen's desire for successful peer relationships. The emphasis here seems to be on the teen's relationship with the therapist. The successful development of the teen's relationship with the therapist—an adult—may itself aid the teen in moving from issues of childhood to the issues of adulthood.

A humanistic therapist might focus primarily on creating a relationship with Mike that would in some ways give the teen a portion of what he is missing from his own family—such as understanding, unconditional positive regard, and empathy. After filling those gaps, Mike could begin to heal. This therapist might also have Mike work out his feelings through expressive pursuits, such as painting, writing, and poetry, to create a safe environment in which to explore solutions to problems. A humanistic therapist offers a nurturing, caring relationship to help deal with the isolation, loneliness, and awkwardness a teen might face.

A behavior therapist is apt to focus on specific problem solving strategies for concerns, such as how Mike could get more time and attention from his father. He or she might set up a system of rewards for Mike's improvement in school. Perhaps this therapist would teach Mike coping skills for mastering each specific problem that came up.

If a teen with a fairly intact personality has behavioral problems—ditching school, being afraid of social interactions, being unable to organize and complete assignments—the behavioral approach might be indicated.

Behavior therapy focuses on specific behavior, such as a youngster's failure to attend classes for the past several weeks. Behavioral techniques may be used to promote motivation and responsibility. They may also be used to work on eliminating or decreasing certain compulsions or phobias that may have other origins.

The eclectic therapist might combine any and all of the above methods. For instance, he or she might talk through Mike's feelings of abandonment by his father but would also work out a system of rewards for school improvement.

An eclectic psychotherapist might talk about early separations and losses, and issues seemingly more remote to the problem at hand. He or she may also use reward systems to motivate the teen to modify his behavior.

The eclectic approach draws on a variety of theories of human behavior. If skillfully employed, it makes use of the best of these approaches in the treatment of an adolescent.

Techniques such as dream analysis or hypnosis may also be used by a therapist to help a teen work through certain conflicts. In some cases where the teen is particularly resistant to therapy and/or may have a limited verbal capacity, media such as art and play may be employed. These methods allow youngsters to express feelings to which they cannot connect verbally.

Family Therapy

Because problems within the family are often at the root of an adolescent's problems, it can be effective—even necessary—to include the family in the therapeutic process. Some therapists may use family therapy in conjunction with individual therapy; others use it as a sole method of treatment. Here is such a case:

> Laura's parents' fighting created more stress than she could take. The fourteen-year-old felt her life had become unbearable.

She feared she might be the cause of their disagreements. Laura was bright and precocious and had dreams of becoming an actress.

So she and a girlfriend decided to run away to New York City. The girls managed to borrow a car, but while still in their state they were pulled over by the police for appearing too young to drive. The school therapist recommended counseling for Laura.

After one session the counselor felt that family therapy was indicated. In a subsequent family session, Laura revealed that even as a preteen she had had to act grown up and to take care of her ill little brother. But now she believed she was being treated like a child.

One of the main advantages of family therapy is that it takes the focus off the adolescent as the identified patient. It addresses the entire family system as a unit in need of improved communication and problem-solving skills. In many instances, therapy with the family seems to be more comfortable and relieving for many teens.

This approach brings to light hidden and even unconscious tensions within the family that are affecting the adolescent. It also allows the therapist to witness "problems" and interactions first-hand, rather than hearing about them through the subjective accounts of the adolescent.

Tension within the parents' relationship may be reflected in the behavior of one of the family members. For example, parents who are always talking about divorce might cause a teen unconsciously to act out in school in order to get into trouble and bring his parents together.

At times an unhealthy family system is kept in balance by maintaining unhealthy behaviors. This is often true of families in which one parent is an alcoholic. In the work of family therapy, this imbalance is identified, and the perceived need to hold on to the parent's drinking problem, for instance, is worked through.

Family therapy is a very specialized skill requiring that the therapist have a variety of sensitivities, talents, and training. A skilled clinician can determine whether a teen would benefit from individual or family therapy alone, or a combination of the two.

Group Therapy

Another modality that may be assessed for the adolescent is group therapy. This approach is particularly appealing to many youngsters because peers and peer relationships are so central in this developmental stage. Such therapy will sometimes be constructed in family modules—for example, a group of four families. Normally, all the people in adolescent group therapy will be youngsters with different or similar problems.

Group therapy may be useful to a teen dealing with substance abuse or with his parent's substance abuse. Group therapy can be used effectively with a teen who is having socialization problems, such as difficulty making friends, dating, succeeding in school, or overcoming other challenges of adolescence. In the following instance, group therapy was very helpful.

> Heather is a fifteen-year-old whose mother became concerned that she had no friends at school. Always painfully shy, Heather experienced additional self-doubt and insecurity when her family moved and she had to change schools. Although she was interested in music and painting and got good grades, Heather was socially shy. At her mother's suggestion, she joined a therapy group for fifteen- and sixteen-year-olds, all of whom had trouble adjusting to high school.
>
> Talking with other students who considered themselves shy helped Heather feel better understood. She received support in working out her problems and felt she could finally relate to other teens and was not alone.

Some teens also seem to take comfort in being with other kids who are dealing with the similar adolescent issues of separation, individuation, peer relationships, and so forth. As in family therapy, the onus in group therapy is removed from the individual. The overall feeling is more one of "we're all in this together." Within group therapy, peers can identify with and relate to the issues that everyone else in the group is experiencing. Teens benefit from each other's feedback, insight, and empathy.

The "group" in group therapy operates within certain parameters. The number of sessions may be predetermined or open-ended. Kids seem to feel some reassurance in facing a finite period of therapy—even if it is as long as one year. The fact that activities other than talking might be part of the process is also appealing to teens.

The group may be composed of diverse individuals. Males and females of varying ages facing different issues may find themselves working together to solve each other's problems. Learning that other teens struggle with similar problems assures teens they are not alone.

Socialization groups can provide a youngster with the ability or the opportunity to learn social and friendship skills in relating to and interacting with peers. Groups of this kind are sometimes offered through community centers, churches, or synagogues, and even through schools. There may be a small fee for participation, but in general, socialization and rap groups are seen as helpful and supportive. They are generally not identified as in-depth therapy groups but as groups that help support adolescents through the stresses and difficulties of that stage of development.

Although the more talkative teens might vie for center stage, a skilled group leader will monitor this and draw out youngsters who are more shy.

A special dynamic and process evolve in each group. Ideally, a sense of camaraderie develops. Group therapy seems especially effective in providing support and help to people who share a similar symptom. When a specific problem—disorders involving eating, substance abuse, or behavior problems—is a focus for all members of the group, more energy can be spent on that common issue.

Group therapy may be prescribed in addition to individual therapy, depending on the therapist's assessment of a youngster's particular need. It is a function of the group therapist to facilitate the group psychodynamic process.

The Initial Assessment

During the initial assessment, the therapist will ask about your youngster's history. Psychological or personality testing may be indicated for any number of reasons. There may be an unclear diagnostic issue. The therapist might use results in planning treatment. He or she may use testing to understand the psychological dynamics of the case.

If a youngster is having problems in school, a therapist may use educational testing to learn his or her scholastic potential, and to help determine whether problems are caused by a learning disability, undue anxiety, or boredom, for instance.

If a therapist suspects that there are underlying problems, unconscious conflicts and difficulties that have not become evident during the consultation, he or she may request that the teen undergo some psychological tests.

Testing may be a particularly threatening experience to many adolescents who fear invasion by adults. A youngster may have exaggerated fears about the power of tests to reveal inner secrets or inadequacies. So great care should be taken when presenting the reason for testing, the nature of the test, and, later, what the results were. Testing can help strengthen a therapist's initial assessment of a problem, and can help him or her estimate the length and nature of treatment. It helps to think of testing as another way of finding answers—or at least learning where to look for them.

There may be adjuncts to therapy, such as self-help groups for alcohol, drug, or food dependencies, which can be important. Group therapy as sort of a support group—for victims of family sexual assault, for instance—can be a valuable adjunct to individual therapy. In chapter 10 and the appendix we will review some of the resources available. It's good to keep all alternatives in mind when discussing your adolescent's plan of treatment.

6

Finding the Right Therapist—Together

Who's the best therapist for your adolescent?

What are the necessary qualifications, background, and training?

How can you best make use of the information you get?

What are the best sources for initial referrals?

How should you evaluate your first phone conversation and/or visit with a therapist?

What questions do you need to ask a potential therapist?

Finding the right mental health professional for your youngster is not a process to be approached randomly or hastily. It requires careful consideration, and cooperation between you and your teen. This chapter will give some concrete guidelines on how to choose a therapist *with* your teenager, not *for* your teenager.

We recommend that you do an in-person interview with at least two or three therapists before you and your youngster make the final determination *together*.

Types of Therapists

When you set out to find the best-trained professional to help your adolescent through his or her problem(s), consider that there are many individuals providing what is commonly called therapy, which may also be referred to as psychotherapy, mental health treatment, or counseling.

These individuals come in all shapes, forms, and sizes, with different academic degrees, training, and licenses. States issue licenses to practice psychology to a number of different types of professionals.

Although people who are not licensed for independent practice can sometimes be valuable in working with adolescents—for example, teachers, clergy, and youth workers—when a teen needs psychotherapy, it is imperative that you find a professional who is licensed by your state to function as an independent practitioner.

Licensing requirements differ from discipline to discipline and from state to state. Most often, to take a state licensing exam, an individual must have an advanced degree from an accredited institution, including specific course work and a number of supervised clinical hours. Licensing exams frequently require successful completion of both written and oral examinations.

Only a percentage of the individuals eligible to take these examinations pass them. In California, for example, to qualify to sit for the psychology examination, a candidate must possess a Ph.D. degree and have completed three thousand hours of supervised training. In 1989 roughly 50 percent of the eligible candidates passed the written exam; of that number, only half passed the oral exam to obtain licensure.

The standard professionals who work with adolescents under state licenses include licensed psychologists; board-certified psychiatrists; licensed marriage, family, and child counselors; and licensed clinical social workers. Licensure requirements may vary from state to state. Though the specific training may differ among these professional groups, most should be certified by the state in which they practice. We recommend that you see a therapist who holds a license or certification.

To help you sort out the alphabet soup of degrees you'll run into when looking for a therapist, we've sketched out brief descriptions of the training qualifications for each professional.

A clinical psychologist is trained to provide psychotherapy, psychodiagnostic assessment, and consultation. A licensed clinical psychologist has completed four to six years of graduate school training, which always includes at least one year of supervised internship.

A doctoral dissertation based on independent research is also required for completion of the Ph.D. degree. The candidate then completes a specified number of supervised postdoctoral hours to enable him or her to sit for the licensing exam.

A psychiatrist is a medical doctor or M.D. who has received specialty training in mental health. After four years of medical school, a psychiatrist goes on to three years of psychiatry residency, which is supervised in both inpatient and outpatient mental health. After residency, the psychiatrist is eligible to sit for board certification in the discipline of psychiatry. He or she is able to prescribe psychotropic medication, as well as to perform psychotherapy. If there is any suspicion of an organic mental problem, or possible need for medication, a psychiatrist should be consulted initially.

Psychiatrists are routinely consulted for medication evaluation, or if a hospitalization is required. Other disciplines also provide hospital treatment.

Master level counselors, including marriage, family, and child counselors, and school, vocational, and pastoral counselors, may be specially trained to work with family problems and other specific issues.

A licensed clinical social worker holds a master of social work (M.S.W.) degree. An L.C.S.W. is usually trained in behavioral sciences and clinical work, both to work within an agency structure, and in some instances to work independently. Social work is the background training, but over the years a substantial component of social casework psychotherapy has been incorporated into this training. Clients may have a strong sociological component, such as economic hardship or physical disability.

All of these degrees require a certain amount of supervised training and experience. The training may be somewhat different in terms of clientele, supervisor, setting, and intensity. However, this does not mean that the selection of the therapist should be based solely on the professional degree.

What's the Difference between Counseling and Therapy?

There is often confusion about the terms *counseling* and *psychotherapy*. They have much in common; counseling, however, generally focuses on specific problems and symptoms, while psychotherapy most often attempts to address underlying issues.

Counseling may be appropriate for people under stressful circumstances. Helping a young person decide such things as what college to attend and what career path to take might be done by a licensed counselor, as opposed to a psychotherapist. A counselor tends to serve as an adviser; whereas a therapist and his or her client often form a more intense relationship to deal with more serious problems.

Counseling is also used when there is a clearly defined problem area or a fairly contained problem. It is frequently time-limited.

Pastoral counselors are usually trained as ministers who are skilled in dealing with spiritual concerns of clients. They also address family and marital problems, and may have training in psychotherapy. Sometimes they serve as good referral sources to other community agencies.

In some cases, paraprofessionals are involved in counseling and therapy. This is usually done in a community setting where there is some training and supervision by a licensed professional.

The key requirement is to find a clinician who is trained to work with adolescents. In looking at the experience of the clinical practitioner, it's best to determine what specific training in working with adolescents that person has had. This information is not always readily available; but when it is not, you should ask in order to determine the extent and quality of prior background.

It is important for parents to be informed consumers when they are choosing a therapist for their adolescent. Be sure to identify whether the therapist has training, experience, and expertise in dealing with adolescents.

Do the Age and Gender of the Therapist Matter?

The age and gender of a therapist can be important, depending upon the type of problem or situation that the adolescent is experiencing. This also may dictate how open and comfortable your teen may be in relation to the therapist.

For example, if the therapist is an elderly man, the young patient may view him as a grandfather, which may allow more of an open, accepting communication, at least initially. On the other hand, certain issues such as sexuality may be difficult for another adolescent to discuss with someone who is considerably older.

Sometimes youngsters can relate better to a younger therapist—even though he or she has less experience than an older one. For instance, your teen may relate and respond better to a thirty-year-old therapist with two years of experience than she would to a person who is fifty-eight and has been in practice for thirty years.

Particularly issues relating to sexuality or peer relationships might be more difficult with too great an age gap between the client and therapist. A therapist who is just a few years older than the teen may not have sufficient authority or maturity in the eyes of the client. The most essential point is the need to be sensitive about the matching of your teen and the therapist. Generally, male teens respond better working with male therapists, and females with female therapists.

The Initial Referral

You may be lucky enough to find an appropriate therapist for your teen by thumbing through the yellow pages. But people usually have far greater success when they obtain recommendations or referrals from people they know. Other professionals may be particularly helpful in evaluating or guiding parents who suspect their teen is in trouble. It's important to turn to these people for assistance and information with regard to referrals. Two good sources of referrals include the pediatrician and family doctor.

Many families in crisis will turn to the physician, who is familiar with and trusted by the family. Depending upon the physician's level of awareness, he or she may be able to assess a psychological problem and recommend a competent therapist, as in these cases:

> Charles, age fourteen, has come in to the doctor's office several times in the last month complaining of stomachaches, headaches, and other somatic complaints. His physician can find no organic origin and discusses with Charlie and his parents the level of stress and conflict that this youngster is experiencing. The doctor subsequently makes a referral to a therapist for a consultation.

> Ling has been losing a lot of weight lately. At fourteen, she is worried about being attractive to boys her age. When her mother arranges for her to see the family doctor, the M.D. determines that the girl's eating behavior has been providing far fewer calories than are needed for her health. Ling has been suffering from anorexia nervosa. A referral is made to a psychologist who specializes in adolescent eating disorders.

In some instances, the physician diagnoses a problem as physical. An example might be various kinds of gastrointestinal problems or other indicators of depression. Physical signs of stress or anxiety such as stomach problems might prompt a concerned physician to refer the family to a psychotherapist.

You and your teen may be unfamiliar with mental health issues and the process and purpose of psychotherapy. Ask your family physician to discuss mental health–related problems with you and to give you some guidance on where to turn.

Another important source of the initial referral is the school. Usually the guidance counselor, dean, principal, and assistant principal are all in a position to make some type of referral for psychological consultation.

For example, if your youngster suddenly shows signs of depression and/or anxiety in the classroom and on the P.E. field with classmates, this may be picked up by school personnel. Most commonly, problems associated with school performance are those that come to the attention of school staff. However, these troubles frequently reflect problems in other areas, including family and peer relations.

More and more officials are being trained and made more aware of potential problems and difficulties that youngsters may be experiencing. Shorter-term, more contained problems are sometimes dealt with by school counselors. However, issues requiring more time-consuming interventions tend to be referred to outside professionals.

The workplace is being provided with employee assistance offers that provide assessment and referral for mental health and chemical dependency; so too there is a new trend toward providing this service in schools.

A priest, minister, rabbi, or other leader familiar with your child might recognize some difficulties within your family or teen or may be called upon when there is a question or potential problem. Most clergy are trained in some form of pastoral counseling and should be able to recognize when there is a need for ongoing help. Cases such as the death of a parent, the stressful breakup of the parents' marriage, a drug problem, or eating disorder, however, may be beyond the scope of what clergy can attend to.

A referral may come from other types of professionals who have some dealings with your family: an adult therapist who is treating another family member, a dentist who recognizes severe anxiety, or a counselor at your workplace who may be consulted when you believe there may be some difficulty with your teen. Referrals can also come from friends, neighbors, family members, or parents of your teen's friends who may have benefited from treatment.

In addition, there are a number of different agencies and organizations in which youngsters are often involved that are familiar with the professional community and can be helpful in providing referrals. These include the YMCA and YWCA, Boys' and Girls' Clubs, and your local community center.

There are also occasions when a referral to a psychotherapist is not an optional one but one mandated by the courts or a law enforcement agency. This is often the case when a youngster has broken the law. Rather than serving time in juvenile hall or a youth camp on a first offense, a teen may be given the opportunity to receive counseling as a diversionary process.

When looking for a therapist for your adolescent, always

Request at least three referrals.

Conduct a preliminary telephone interview.

Interview in person with your teen the two or three most promising potential therapists before making a decision to work with one.

Making That Initial Contact with a Therapist

There are a number of areas in which parents and their adolescent must feel comfortable before proceeding with therapy. Your first contact with a therapist will usually be by phone—a call you make based ideally on a reliable referral. You'll want to determine at the outset whether he or she works with adolescents on a regular basis.

For the most part, therapists can be informative about how they have approached problems similar to your teen's. The initial telephone contact can indicate a good deal about the therapist's communication style and the potential for a good relationship between therapist, teen, and parent(s).

Your first conversation with a therapist is likely to tell you a lot about the therapist's personality, and whether he or she would be helpful, concerned, and "on the same wavelength" as you and your youngster. To aid you further in screening for the best therapist for your youngster, we have included questions at the end of this chapter that you will want to ask yourself and the therapist.

How comfortable and at ease you feel during this first phone or in-person contact is an important indicator. As a rule, follow your instinct. Here are the general steps to an efficient first phone contact:

1. Identify yourself and the referral source.
2. Tell your therapist your youngster's age and gender, and briefly describe your youngster's problem and what you hope therapy might accomplish.

This second step will allow a therapist to tell you whether he or she can treat the problem or can recommend a better source. If a therapist does not specialize in the eating disorder your daughter has been diagnosed with, finding out by phone can save you time, money, and frustration.

In other instances, the specialty area is less important than overall knowledge and skill in being able to work well with adolescents in a general way.

Strive to become an informed consumer of a process that is likely to be key in your teen's development—and possibly survival. Even if you are at your wits' end by the time you reach the point of seeking therapy—as many parents are—spending this energy will pay off for you and your teenager.

You'll probably want to ask up front what the therapist's fee is, and whether or not he or she accepts insurance. There should be no discomfort or hesitation on the therapist's part. Some therapists accept payment in full for their services at the time of each visit. Others are willing to bill monthly. Some have the insurance company reimburse the client. Others are willing to have the insurance company pay them directly. Some therapists will work on a sliding fee scale. These financial issues need to be clarified once you become interested in having this therapist see your teen.

You can find out in the initial phone conversation who needs to be present at the first session and how long the sessions are. If your teen will be getting to appointments on his or her own, you may ask about public transportation to the office. Because the initial meeting can be difficult and anxiety provoking, it's a good idea to have precise directions to the office, to prevent unnecessary stress.

What Does the First Session Involve?

Knowing what to expect during your first face-to-face visit with a therapist and what questions to ask can decrease anxiety and make the process run more smoothly. Even if individual therapy is indicated, it is common that the therapist will ask the entire family—or at least the parent(s) and teen—to attend the first session together.

When you make your first visit to the therapist's office, a number of things need to be taken into consideration. Does the family feel comfortable and secure in the office? Are the furnishings and overall environment appealing to a teenager? Is there a quality of general professionalism about the appearance of the office and the therapist?

It is important for both you and your teen to be able to develop a professional relationship with the therapist you have selected together. Both parties need to feel understood by the therapist in terms of the family crisis at hand and the pain and difficulty experienced from your perspective and your teen's. Feeling understood will create a sense of security and safety for the entire family, and the real work of exploring the problem of finding solutions can begin.

It is reasonable to expect at the conclusion of this first visit that the therapist will make some statement about recommendations for treatment, and about how he or she plans to proceed should you decide to pursue that professional relationship.

You will be interested in finding out how the therapist would approach working with your teen. Not all of your questions may be answerable during the first session. This time is usually spent getting to know the therapist, assessing the problem, and setting out some preliminary treatment plan.

We cannot stress enough how vital it is that your teen be included in this decision. Ideally, the therapist is a person with whom your son or daughter will form a trusting, enduring relationship. Teens rarely warm up immediately to the idea of seeing a therapist. Indeed, sometimes parents and kids battle over the decision quite a bit.

Your teen may dislike every therapist you suggest, causing you to want to make the decision for him or her. Perhaps the best approach to take with a reluctant teen is to point out that he or she *is* going to talk to somebody, and that you want your teen to share in the selection process so that he or she will be as content as possible with the therapist. When your teen feels a certain level of comfort, control, and understanding, a stronger, more effective therapeutic alliance can be formed.

Making the Selection

Questions to Ask a Potential Therapist

Before trusting your adolescent to a particular therapist, you will want to screen potential therapists ahead of time—by phone or, if possible, in a face-to-face interview. Here are some questions you may want to ask:

1. Have you been trained formally to work with adolescents?
2. What has been your training in working with teens who have problems similar to my child's?
3. Are you licensed to practice therapy?
4. What has been your experience?
5. What is your therapeutic orientation?
6. How do you work with kids like my son or daughter?
7. What role would you expect the parents to play in our child's therapy?
8. What are your fees?
9. Do you accept insurance?
10. Do you charge for an initial telephone conversation? Do you charge for an initial meeting?
11. Do you work on a sliding scale (when applicable)?
12. How frequently would you plan on meeting with my teen?
13. Does this seem to be a problem that will require short-term or extended therapy?
14. Do our schedules match?
15. What is your policy regarding telephone contact?
16. Can we or our teen call you between sessions?

Questions Families Ask Themselves during an Interview

You begin to form a relationship with a therapist during the first contact, be that by phone or in person. When interviewing a therapist, trust your own feelings. Even if you do the initial screening of several therapists, it's essential that you and your adolescent participate in the final selection of the therapist.

After the family interviews a therapist together, be sure to discuss the feelings you had about each therapist together and work on agreeing on one. Here are some sample questions parents and adolescents might ask themselves while interviewing a potential therapist:

1. Do I like this person?
2. Does this therapist have an appealing personality?
3. Does therapist seem to understand me?
4. Is this someone I would feel comfortable confiding in?
5. Do I respect this person?
6. If the therapist is the same sex as your teen, will he or she be seen as a good role model?
7. If he or she is of the opposite sex, will that fact create a barrier?
8. Is the office easy to get to, if necessary, by public transportation?
9. Is there a sense of warmth and professionalism about this person?
10. Does the office look as if it would be comfortable for a teen? (If it's too shabby, your teen might not feel good about going there. If the office is too formal, your teen may feel uneasy.)
11. Is the office set up so that my adolescent will not have to run into people in the waiting room, should this be a problem?
12. Is the therapist well groomed and neat?
13. Does he or she seem aware of adolescent issues and concerns?

7

Understanding the Therapeutic Process

What does it mean that my teen needs therapy?

What goes on behind the therapist's doors?

Will my youngster be revealing family secrets?

What kind of changes can I expect?

How long will it take before I see results?

Will all of my teen's problems be solved through therapy?

What *can't* therapy accomplish?

How can I be sure something is being accomplished?

How can I keep from feeling left out of the therapy process?

Will my teen turn against me?

Will the therapist become more important to my child than I am?

How will I know when it's time to end therapy?

What changes might take place in my teen?

What are some of the benefits of therapy?

Part of what can make getting help from a professional seem difficult—be it an accountant to help solve your tax problems or a dentist to fix your teeth—lies in fear of the unknown.

Therapy has a beginning, middle, and end. And it can be a positive, growth-promoting experience that will give your adolescent vital coping tools that will serve him or her throughout life. But even if you're convinced of this, not knowing what to expect can be confusing.

Initial Concerns

Kids Fear They're Being Punished

Therapy is not the giving of advice, the administration of punishment, or the passing of judgment, though teens may perceive it as all of these. After all, it tends to be initiated by parents, sometimes with a push from school officials, a family doctor, or a law enforcement agency. A teen's sense of being intruded upon or punished can initially be very strong.

If a therapist were to ask a young patient, "Why are you here?" the answer might be something like, "Because I got suspended from school," "Because my parents made me come here," or "I'm a screw-up." In other words, teens often have the perception that they are in therapy because they did something wrong or are bad. To improve the chances of therapy's success, it's vital that it not be presented as a punishment or negative consequence to your teen.

For adolescents, the search for a therapist has often been warranted by a specific behavioral problem, such as poor school performance or behavior, substance abuse, or delinquent behavior. The therapeutic process generally aims as well at addressing underlying and long-standing issues.

Teens May Initially Resist Therapy

Therapy is not magical, nor is it a cure-all or panacea. What therapy does provide is a process of healing, guidance, and help for particular problems and/or situations.

In fact all clients—young children, adolescents, and adults—seem to resist therapy initially, even when they have voluntarily sought help. Resistance can be viewed as an inevitable part of the process of confronting painful truths. It takes time for an alliance to form between a therapist and client. And this can be particularly stormy and stressful when working with an adolescent.

In addition to the types of resistance all therapy clients share, resistance for a teenager may be caused by a number of different factors. To begin with, no one likes to be forced into therapy, but this is often the case with teenagers. It may also have to do with why the adolescent feels he or she is being "forced" to talk to a stranger for help. For example, failing in school or not getting along with family or peers may not seem like a big deal to a teen. To a youngster the therapist may appear to be just another oppressive authority figure, trying to intrude upon his or her life. A teen may perceive that she is being "sent" to therapy because her parents and the therapist think she is "crazy" or a "problem." Resistance may also reflect a denial that any problem exists.

Part of a youngster's resistance may be an avoidance of certain important issues that he or she is denying, suppressing, or hiding. A teen may fear that he or she will "flunk" therapy. A good therapist balances the building of trust and support within the therapeutic process with confrontation of those issues.

A teen may have fears about what is expected of him or her, or about what is supposed to be accomplished in therapy. Since adolescence is normally a time of increasing independence from parents, the pressure of working on problems with an adult may be construed as an invasion of the youngster's privacy. Since teens so often guard their privacy in issues of sexuality and peer relationships, opening up to a therapist can be difficult.

Resistance is expressed in many forms. One of the most obvious forms of resistance is missing or forgetting a session. Teens often create conflicting obligations, forget sessions, or show up late to demonstrate ambivalent feelings about therapy.

Getting Therapy Off to a Good Start

Overcoming Resistance

To help a teen overcome his or her resistance, a therapist might start by talking about less threatening subjects that still have relevance to the important issues. If it's difficult for a teenager to discuss his parents' divorce and how much he misses his father, the therapist might start talking to the teen about sports, which could then lead the youngster to discuss how he and his father used to go to ball games together.

The therapist may say that he shares the teen's enthusiasm for baseball and use this shared interest to begin to understand how the teen thinks and feels about other aspects of life. A good therapist will establish with the teen that he or she is interested in the youngster as a person—not just in correcting a perceived problem. The therapist will communicate a desire to understand the teen, and to help interpret what may be going on in his or her life and mind. The therapist may discuss how hard it is to talk about how much he misses being with his dad, thus interpreting the resistance.

Generating the Therapeutic Alliance

It is quite natural for parents to define their youngster's problem differently from the way the teen does. Teens often minimize or avoid the more painful aspects of their circumstances and assume that no adult could possibly understand what they are going through. This is where the skill of the therapist is crucial in making it safe for the adolescent to reveal his or her feelings more freely.

The trusting relationship between the youngster and the therapist begins to form. It is also essential that the young client feel that the therapist understands him or her as a person, and not just as someone with a problem. A therapist might not entirely agree but needs to let the teen know his or her opinion is valid. In some cases, the therapist is the first person who has listened or seemed to side with the teen, from the youngster's perspective.

One of the cornerstones of therapy is the fact that we tend to experience adult figures as we experienced our parents. Adolescent therapy can be complicated by the fact that kids often distrust adults—including the therapist. So the teen may see the therapist in a parental role, which all too often conjures up negative feelings. This is a fairly normal characteristic of the beginning of therapy, and it should decrease as the teen becomes more comfortable with the therapist.

The alliance within therapy may differ from individual to individual. Rarely there may be almost instant bonding. More often it takes place over a period of weeks or months. As the process unfolds, teens tend to be more willing—even eager—to attend sessions. The perceived value of therapy increases. And behavior starts to change.

As the alliance strengthens, the adolescent begins to accept input from the therapist more willingly and feels less that it is distorted, inaccurate, or critical. The communication between the therapist and the client becomes a model for what is possible in human communication, and it therefore begins to set the tone for improved communication at home and with peers.

Carl Rogers created the term *unconditional positive regard.* A therapist can help a youngster improve his or her self-esteem by giving certain positive messages and helping to correct distortions in the youngster's thinking. Here is a teen who needs to hear some positive messages:

> "My teachers pick on me because I'm stupid," fourteen-year-old Nathan complained to his therapist. "Nobody likes me because I'm stupid, and I hate myself."

Nathan's therapist used comments like these: "You are a good person," "I like you and enjoy being with you," and "You are loved by your family." He also discussed how Nathan has shown success in several areas. By learning to use such resources as his basketball coach, the school peer counselor, and his minister, Nathan learned to express, channel, and direct his feelings, and he eventually grew to believe that people did like him and that he was intelligent.

As trust develops, the therapist tries to teach and promote the use of insight by the adolescent in terms of looking at certain situations or problems, and connecting his or her feelings to these behaviors. In some ways a therapist becomes a teacher or a guide.

Ideally, a therapist will become a youngster's ally and will help him or her understand and control behaviors that are troubling.

The therapist will also interpret situations that are frightening and confusing.

Confidentiality: The Blurred but Sacred Line

Once resistance starts to decrease and a youngster begins to respond to therapy, he or she will gradually open up and begin sharing thoughts and feelings with the therapist, which will eventually lead to solutions.

Because your teen is a minor, you are legally entitled to information that would not be considered ethical for an adult's therapist to divulge. You need to trust the professionalism and judgment of a therapist to convey what is necessary while letting a lot remain private between your teen and the therapist. Before therapy begins, all parties need to understand and agree that the sessions will be confidential.

Parents Need to Trust

A therapist needs to create a feeling of safety, security, and privacy within the office. In the beginning, a teen will undoubtedly fear that the therapist is in cahoots with the parents and will "betray" or reveal to the parents what goes on behind the therapy doors. A teen may view the therapist as the agent of the parents, delving into the darkest secrets, fears, and concerns of the teen. Such fears need to be dispelled during the initial sessions.

As much as possible, when you need to talk with the therapist about your adolescent, issues should be discussed with the youngster present. In advance of any meetings you have with the therapist alone, the therapist and your teen should discuss what will be revealed and what information the teen considers inviolable.

Parents sometimes feel excluded from the inner workings of the therapeutic process. But unless they view the relationship between the teen and therapist as private to a degree, therapy will be of limited value. If a teen is a danger to himself or others, however, or if child abuse is suspected, state laws require no confidentiality within the therapeutic process.

For the most part, parents of adolescents in therapy need to accept the idea that their role is to support a relationship with another adult that allows for a freer exploration of life's issues at that developmental stage than is usually possible with parents. If therapy is to be effective, the parents' knowledge of the specific content of each session will be limited. Sometimes, a therapist will advise a family session.

> Linda, fourteen, felt great anger toward her sixteen-year-old sister, whom she believed her parents favored. She claimed her parents always sided with her sister and "attacked" her point of view.

Linda's therapist might ask her if it's all right to bring her family in to talk about some of her concerns during a family session. In essence, the therapist asks a teen's permission to allow the family to become involved.

Show Me Results!

Undoubtedly parents want to see tangible results from their child's therapy. Just as you go to a medical doctor and expect to have your symptoms relieved, so it is with therapy. But results are rarely immediate. It is reasonable for you to expect, over the course of several months, to see signs of improvement and progress. These improvements tend to occur most readily in social relationships, then at school, and finally at home. Your youngster's progress may be discussed with you and your child, and periodic assessments may be made along the way.

Parents and teens establish trust in their therapist. Progress should be expected. Symptoms diminish. Behavior and feelings should change. Therapy should not go on forever.

At first you may have to keep a keen eye out for improvement in your teen. You might see a greater level of confidence, increased self-esteem, improved ability to solve problems within the family and social circle, decreased anger, better control of impulses, and greater feelings of hope that life's problems can be solved.

Overall, the goal of therapy is quite specific to each youngster and his or her family. Generally you're aiming for improved functioning in love, work, and play, which should lead to improved self-esteem.

In adolescent therapy, the therapist often becomes a model for the youngster of how to function competently and even to thrive in the world. The emphasis in therapy is not just on modeling a teen's behavior, but also on understanding and developing directions that foster future adult functioning.

It is important to note that a youngster's improvement may not be consistent. Steps backward may occur, and a teen may express anger and frustration during a particular stormy period.

In time, however, a youngster may come to feel that each therapy session is a positive experience in which important work is accomplished. There will be some sessions that are more difficult than others, and your youngster's mood may reflect frustration. But overall the therapeutic process generates a feeling of progress. Your teen may eventually look forward to airing troubling feelings and working problems out.

What Changes Might Occur at Home?

When your teen comes home from a therapy session, you may notice attitudinal changes. Your youngster will be developing greater self-esteem, improving confidence, and becoming more assertive and expressive.

8

Getting Involved with Your Teen's Therapy

The Family Does *Make a Difference*

How can my family get involved with my teen's therapy?

In what other ways can the family help?

If my youngster doesn't seem to listen to me anyway, what good is my involvement?

Dropping your youngster off for therapy does not mean handing him over, body and soul, to the therapist. In fact, with the help of a professional, your role can be even more vital and effective. Even though someone else will aid you, your youngster still needs your love, encouragement, and support. Therapy often opens lines of communication among family members and increases the whole family's potential.

You may be involved at times in your teen's actual treatment or simply be supportive of him or her. Among the various roles you can play in your youngster's therapy are these:

Keep a supportive attitude toward your teen's difficulties and sometimes frustrating process of change.

Be available to talk when your teen wants to discuss things (but not pushy).

Participate in periodic family meetings if that is desired by your teen and therapist.

Attend to such mundane things as providing transportation if needed. Be careful not to schedule conflicting activities that would interfere with therapy.

When an individual or family comes in for consultation, it helps if all participating members of the family share a similar concept of why they are there. But sometimes the willingness to seek help is the only thing that parents and teens agree upon at the time.

Even when your teen is in individual therapy, the therapist may ask other family members to be involved because the family is looked upon as a system. If the system is off balance, other issues may be addressed. Here is one such case:

> The older brother of sixteen-year-old Jason was killed in a car accident. In grief counseling, Jason told his therapist that he wanted to die. He had lost interest in the joys of life. Because the whole family was affected by the older boy's death, the whole family was involved in therapy. In this case the best thing Jason's parents were able to do was to get some counseling for themselves. The family members were better able to work through their grief together.

As the treatment process progresses, you may be asked to come in for occasional sessions alone, with your spouse, or with other family members. Sometimes in these meetings specific conflicts will be addressed. Or you may simply be given an update on the progress of your youngster's treatment. This is most desirable when done with your teen present, or at least when discussed with him or her in advance.

Besides being actively involved in your teen's healing process, you can be supportive of his or her efforts:

Be as open as possible with your teen.

Make an effort to listen.

Respect his or her privacy.

Pay attention to changes taking place within your youngster and the family.

9

Progress, Resolution, and Conclusion

How will I know when my youngster is ready to end therapy?

Can my teen go back to the therapist if another problem arises?

Have my teen's major problems been sufficiently resolved?

Is there no impending crisis in my youngster or in our family situation?

Does my youngster seem happier?

Does my teen appear more calm and understanding?

Does my teen have better relationships with family members and friends?

Is my youngster making progress in school achievement?

Has my teen's behavior improved?

Does my youngster have a more positive, open attitude?

Does my teen communicate better?

Has my youngster's overall functioning improved?

Have I noticed growth and maturity?

"Getting better" through therapy is not always a clear-cut moment but an invisible healing process. It is rarely the dramatic and obvious "cure" or completion of problems that we want it to be. It is more apt to be a gradual improvement that diminishes the pain caused by certain problems. There simply comes a point where the problem for which a client initially sought therapy has more or less been resolved. The decision is then made either to move on to other areas of concern or to consider the therapy process completed.

The process of therapy may have become completely enlightening and uplifting to the adolescent as well as to the family, as in this case:

> Thirteen-year-old Dean has been in therapy for a year. His parents have attended some joint sessions and are now very pleased about their son's progress. Not only has his school performance improved, but he seems to be making more friends. He is getting along better with his father and seems happier overall. The mutual decision is made to end therapy.

Beware of the "Flight into Health"

At times a teen may have premature feelings that things are going better and therapy should end. The adolescent may have shown some positive change in attitudes, behavior, and performance, and a decrease in symptoms.

Sometimes at the first sign of improvement a teen and/or the parents may find that the desire to be "healthy," or the fear of therapy or of becoming dependent on therapy, is so strong that the youngster pretends to recover instantly. This happens more frequently with adolescents than with adults, so we urge caution in looking at the need for a fairly deliberate step-by-step resolution of major problems in this stage of development.

For instance, problems involving school performance, peer relationships, and substance abuse do not vanish instantly. It may be important for the therapist in measuring a youngster's progress to be particularly aware that it is not always just the decrease of symptoms to which one pays attention but the likelihood that the causes of the symptoms have really been resolved.

A teen should continue to exhibit improvement consistently

for a period of time before parents assume that the problem has been adequately resolved. Improvement in family and peer relationships, school performance, and self-confidence should be evident not just fleetingly but over a period of time.

Sometimes parents and teens become concerned that the teen will become dependent on therapy, and that the longer therapy goes on, the less he or she will be able to function without it.

But that fear is contrary to the goal of therapy, which ultimately promotes more independent functioning. Remember, a therapist does not give answers; rather, the therapist guides the adolescent in his or her own search. One of the things therapy tries to do is promote internal responsibility for one's own life and actions. What therapy accomplishes, ideally, are internal changes that are permanent.

Internal guidance, direction, restraint, and insight replace external controls. This occurs naturally in the normal adolescent process. Psychotherapy can help facilitate this experience and can also help adolescents who are having difficulty avoiding some destructive side trips on this journey. Therapy instills problem-solving skills and improves self-esteem and self-confidence.

Conclusion of Therapy

The timing of the end of therapy is important in many ways. While it is a relief to have fewer and less intense problems, the loss of an important person—the therapist—is not taken lightly by a teen. A youngster is ready to end therapy when he or she has implemented the major lessons learned in therapy. A teen, the parents, and the therapist should all agree on a comfortable stopping point.

The goal of a therapist is to conclude the relationship with his or her client on as healthy and positive a note as possible.

As therapy is winding down, issues of abandonment, loss, and separation sometimes surface and need to be addressed. It is important that a teen know he or she can return to therapy for a "tune-up" should other issues or problems arise.

A teen may react to the termination of therapy with anger,

depression, or denial, because it means leaving someone to whom he or she has formed a significant attachment. Because therapy has become a valued experience, leaving it can be difficult.

A teen may feel abandoned by the therapist. So he or she may want to terminate therapy the moment the possibility of ending therapy is mentioned. This may indicate that the teen wants to abandon the therapist before the therapist abandons him or her. This reaction should be discouraged. However, the feelings should be thoroughly expressed, explored, and discussed. The purpose of therapy is to express thoughts and feelings without acting out.

One of the most important and valuable things that can take place toward the end of therapy is the review of what has happened over the course of treatment. The good feelings between the adolescent and therapist are reinforced. The fact that positive change has occurred is recognized. Doors are left open for future contact with and support by the therapist. The conclusion of therapy can be viewed as a graduation of sorts and should be celebrated.

10

Knowing Your Alternatives

What alternatives do I have to therapy?

What is the value of self-help groups?

What can I do for my teen's drug problem?

When might hospitalization be indicated?

What is inpatient hospitalization like?

Aside from private therapists, there are other routes you may want to consider when seeking help for your adolescent. Obviously, private therapy alone is not the answer to all problems. Certain challenges, such as severe drug abuse, an eating disorder, or psychotic breakdown, may require additional intervention.

If you're concerned that there may be something seriously wrong with your youngster, you can go to a psychiatrist or psychologist for a consultation for a specific diagnosis. The consultant may recommend a treatment alternative and/or an adjunctive service.

These treatment alternatives include intensive outpatient, chemical dependency, psychiatric, and inpatient chemical dependency, as well as various self-help groups, residential treatment, day treatment, and inpatient hospitalization.

A consulting therapist can determine what's wrong, what kind of help you can get, and where you can go for it. A therapist may tell you that your youngster does not need therapy but may need to enroll in special education classes, receive further testing, or undergo inpatient treatment for a drug problem.

Self-Help Groups

Often in conjunction with individual or family therapy, self-help groups can be beneficial. These groups provide ongoing support and help with symptom management in relation to substance abuse. There are supportive groups that exist for teenage drug abusers and kids with a family member who abuses drugs. These generally make use of a twelve-step program similar to that used by Alcoholics Anonymous. These groups are focused on cocaine, narcotics, overeating, gambling, debt, and the like. Groups are now forming for youngsters with severe anxiety and dysfunctional families.

Intensive Outpatient Treatment

This type of treatment is simply an intensification of the therapy process. If a youngster is in a temporary crisis situation, it may be determined that it would be helpful to increase the number of sessions, institute some family sessions, or add medication. This method attempts to intervene while the teen remains at home with the family.

> Randy had been in therapy for a few months when his best friend was killed in an auto accident. Randy became very seriously depressed, though not suicidal. It was decided to increase therapy from once to twice a week for a time.

Some intensive outpatient programs are focused on chemical dependency, eating, or anxiety disorders. The intensive outpatient method attempts to intervene without resorting to an inpatient hospitalization and is preferable in many cases, like this one:

> Kelly, seventeen, had been using drugs for two years. Several inpatient stays, during which she was removed from her environment and then placed back in it after thirty days, had not been effective; she didn't follow her aftercare programs and continued to return to using drugs.

Her therapist recommended that Kelly become involved in an intensive outpatient program so that she could still attend school but would attend several group meetings per week and would be followed by her individual counselor. This program better enabled her to maintain sobriety.

Inpatient Hospitalization

This treatment can be helpful in a variety of situational crises. When a teen poses some harm to him- or herself or to others, inpatient treatment may be warranted. A youngster with suicidal tendencies may require a period of inpatient hospitalization.

Phase One: It may be determined what is required to keep the teen safe. A youngster with suicidal tendencies may temporarily require care in a locked facility or be placed with a twenty-four-hour companion.

Phase Two: The therapist or hospital official may try to identify the central problems.

Phase Three: The therapist will establish a treatment plan during the teen's hospital stay, working with the staff treatment team. Medication may be prescribed and coordinated within the treatment.

Phase Four: Plans regarding follow-up once the teen leaves the hospital may be outlined.

Some acute crises that involve violence or threats of violence, such as assaulting a teacher, setting a classroom on fire, or destroying a living room in a fit of rage, may also necessitate an inpatient stay. A youngster who poses a risk to himself may require a locked facility and a suicide watch.

Inpatient hospitalization may be voluntary—recommended by the therapist and agreed upon by the youngster and parents. If you're considering a voluntary stay in the hospital, seek a consultation with a knowledgeable professional in the field. You can certainly get a second opinion, as Laura's parents did:

Seventeen-year-old Laura has been involved with marijuana and alcohol use. The first therapist consulted wants to admit her to a hospital right away. Her parents get a second opinion from another therapist, who suggests starting treatment with intensive outpatient work, which also involves family therapy. Her parents have the choice to go with the option with which they are most comfortable.

Inpatient treatment may also be indicated in cases where psychotic symptoms and functioning are present, such as when a youngster hears voices telling him to jump off a building, or when someone becomes completely withdrawn and lethargic and begins talking to an imaginary person. Hospitalization may also be recommended in cases of severe drug or alcohol abuse or for eating disorders, such as bulimia and anorexia nervosa.

The presence of an eating disorder or drug problem does not necessarily demand inpatient treatment, but it may require consultation with a professional to determine whether it is preferable to outpatient care or to intensive outpatient treatment. A detox center may be necessary in some cases, followed by referral to outpatient treatment.

How Inpatient Treatment Can Help

Hospitalization can provide help and support for a youngster and his or her family at a particularly stressful time. Even if the home environment is loving and supportive, a teen may reject one or both parents or other elements at home, and he or she will respond better to receiving help in a safe hospital environment.

Not only can hospitalization prevent more serious consequences of a trauma or crisis, but it can also promote a more intensive therapeutic experience; and that can be helpful and necessary in resolving the specific trauma or situation. Seeing a therapist daily, being in an ongoing group, and having medical staff involved and available at all times can be very therapeutic to a troubled teen. An adolescent thinking seriously about suicide, for example, may need this kind of intensive treatment.

Juan, a youngster who over the past several months has become more withdrawn, spends all day in his room. He doesn't want to go out. His parents fear that if he stays at home, he might kill himself. He has written letters talking about death and outlining suicide with a plan.

Before the patient is checked into the hospital, a psychiatric evaluation will be done by a professional. This will help determine the teen's mental status, severity of the problem(s), psychosocial factors, history, potential risk, and treatment recommendation.

There are fears and apprehensions attached to hospitalization for anything. Here are some questions you can ask before your teen is admitted to the hospital:

What is the purpose of hospitalization?

What will my youngster be doing?

What is the anticipated length of stay?

Who will be working with my teen?

What will my involvement be?

Can I visit my youngster?

How can I help and support?

What Takes Place during Hospitalization?

Upon admission, a youngster and his or her family are typically given an initial assessment. The youngster is assigned a room, which he or she will usually share with another teen child. More and more hospitals are forming inpatient adolescent units that strictly gear their programs toward adolescent treatment. A school program is usually offered as part of the hospitalization. Youngsters who've made some progress may be taken out to schools in the area and brought back to the hospital at night.

Residential Treatment

Usually this treatment involves a long-term placement, where the youngster lives with other kids in a therapeutic setting. This is often indicated in cases where there is severe family dysfunction or abuse or severe disturbance, or where the adolescent's problems are such that they cannot be adequately treated in the family setting. There may also have been repeated involvement with law enforcement, and a judge may have ruled out juvenile detention or imprisonment.

Residential treatment is very expensive and at times may be funded by the state through the courts or Department of Children's Services. The goal is to maintain the youngster in a structured therapeutic setting.

In residential treatment, the length of stay is usually from several months to several years. For the most part, residential facilities attempt to involve families in their programs and may include visitation and family therapy as part of the integration of the program. Residential treatment is frequently used in cases where severe delinquent acts raise concern about future criminal activity. The family may be so dysfunctional that major intervention in the whole family system is needed, and the adolescent must live apart from the family.

Occasionally, instead of sending a youngster to juvenile hall or a juvenile camp for committing a crime, a judge may recommend residential treatment. This alternative is considered when the problem seems to be more related to some form of family disruption and/or a psychological component than to the incident and the offense committed.

Drug Treatment Centers

There are many drug treatment centers around the country that specifically offer services to adolescent substance abusers. We list several specific resources in the appendix. Frequently these programs work in conjunction with self-help groups such as Alcoholics Anonymous and Narcotics Anonymous. These centers rely heavily on the value of a contained environment to help an adolescent overcome both a physical dependency on drugs or alcohol and the peer pressure to use the substance.

The severity of the addiction is perhaps the key factor in determining whether or not inpatient treatment is an appropriate intervention. In certain extreme cases where chemical dependency is at stake, a period of inpatient care may be required for detoxification.

Other determinations in terms of the assessment of the drug involvement and the severity of the addiction include how self-destructive a youngster is, and what symptoms he or she displays—such as stealing to support a drug habit. All of these may be indicators of a fairly severe addiction that needs attention and may require hospitalization.

There are programs that are strictly for drug rehab. Others incorporate treatment for other disorders, such as depression. Usually the family is involved with the therapist and the program administrators throughout the hospital stay. In some cases an intensive outpatient program may be a more appropriate alternative.

After a youngster is discharged from the hospital, there is usually an aftercare program provided by the facility. A youngster may become involved in one or more support groups. There is usually follow-up by the therapist who treated the teen during his or her hospital stay.

Inpatient treatment is also used for life-threatening eating disorders where medical intervention is needed. These programs are generally patterned after the drug and alcohol abuse programs, and usually include the same components of medical, psychiatric, and family therapy.

You'll Always Be Your Youngster's Parent

You've tuned into recognizing whether your teen is going through a harmless phase or needs professional attention. You are familiar with different types of therapy and other resources that are available. And you know how to make the best use of them. Most of all, you're in the right frame of mind to be of the greatest help to your youngster when he or she really needs you. It's likely that whatever problems your teen is experiencing are only temporary. And you're doing something to ensure that. Remember, no matter how grown up your adolescent acts or seems, he or she is still your child and right now needs you more than ever.

Appendix:

Further Resources Available to You

Adoption

Adoptees' Liberty Movement Association
P.O. Box 154
Washington Bridge Station
New York, NY 10033
(212) 581-1568

Liberal Education for Adoptive Families
23247 Lofton Court North
Scandia, MN 55073
(612) 636-7031

National Adoption Information Exchange System
67 Irving Place
New York, NY 10003
(212) 254-7410

National Right to Life Committee
National Press Building
529 Fourteenth Street NW, No. 341
Washington, DC 20045
(202) 638-4396

North American Center on Adoption
67 Irving Place
New York, NY 10003
(212) 254-7410

Volunteers of America
3939 North Causeway Boulevard, Suite 202
Metairie, LA 70002
(504) 837-2652

Waif
67 Irving Place
New York, NY 10003
(212) 533-2558

Alcoholism and Drug Abuse

Al-Anon Family Group Headquarters
1372 Broadway
New York, NY 10018
(212) 302-7240

Alcohol and Drug Abuse Prevention Network
Office of Juvenile Justice and Delinquency Prevention
Department of Justice
Washington, DC 20530
(202) 724-5911

Alcohol and Drug Problems Association of North America
1101 Fifteenth Street NW
(202) 452-0990

Alcohol Education for Youth
1500 Western Avenue
Albany, NY 12203
(518) 456-3800

Alcoholics Anonymous World Services
P.O. Box 459, Grand Central Station
New York, NY 10163
(212) 686-1100

Alcoholism Center for Women
1147 South Alvarado Street
Los Angeles, CA 90006
(213) 381-7805

American Council on Alcohol Problems
3426 Bridgeland Drive
Bridgeton, MO 63044

American Medical Society on Alcoholism
733 Third Avenue
New York, NY 10017
(212) 986-4433

Association of Halfway House Alcoholism Programs
of North America
786 East Seventh Street
St. Paul, MN 55106
(612) 771-0933

Do It Now Foundation
P.O. Box 27568
Tempe, AZ 85285
(602) 491-0393

Hazelden Foundation
P.O. Box 11
Center City, MN 55012
(612) 257-4010

International Commission for the Prevention of Alcoholism
6840 Eastern Avenue
Washington, DC 20012
(202) 723-0800

International Halfway House Association
500 North Washington Street
Alexandria, VA 22314
(703) 594-7202

National Association of Alcoholism Treatment Programs
2415 South 2300 West
Salt Lake City, UT 84119
(801) 972-6141

National Clergy Council on Alcoholism and Related Drug Problems
3112 Seventh Street NE
Washington, DC 20017
(202) 832-3811

National Committee for the Prevention of Alcoholism and Drug Dependency
6830 Laurel Street NW
Washington, DC 20012
(202) 723-4774

National Council on Alcoholism
12 West Twenty-first Street
New York, NY 10017
(212) 206-6770

National Listen America Club
7545 Jurupa Avenue
Riverside, CA 92504
(714) 688-2301

Prevention Resource Center
901 South Second Street
Springfield, IL 62704
(217) 525-3456

DRUG ABUSE

Addiction Research and Treatment Corporation
22 Chapel Street
Brooklyn, NY 11201
(212) 834-5300

Alcohol and Drug Problems Association of North America
1101 Fifteenth Street, NW
Washington, DC 20005
(202) 452-0990

American Council on Marijuana and Other
Psychoactive Drugs
136 East Sixty-fourth Street
New York, NY 10021
(212) 758-8060

Anti-Drug Coalition
304 West Fifty-eighth Street
New York, NY 10019
(212) 247-8820

Center for the Study of Drug Policy
530 Eighth Street SE
Washington, DC 20003
(202) 547-3708

Citizens for Informed Choices on Marijuana
300 Broad Street
Stamford, CT 06901
(203) 324-3636

Families Anonymous
P.O. Box 344
Torrance, CA 90501
(213) 775-3211

Families in Action
P.O. Box 15053
Atlanta, GA 30333
(404) 378-3310

International Narcotic Enforcement Officers Association
112 State Street, Suite 1310
Albany, NY 12207
(518) 463-6232

Narcotic Educational Foundation of America
5055 Sunset Boulevard
Los Angeles, CA 90027
(213) 663-5171

Narcotics Anonymous
P.O. Box 9999
Van Nuys, CA 91409
(818) 780-3951

Narcotics Education, Inc.
Laurel Street NW
Washington, DC 20012
(202) 723-4774

National Association on Drug Abuse Problems
355 Lexington Avenue
New York, NY 10017
(212) 986-1170

National Association of State Alcohol and
Drug Abuse Directors
1336 New York Avenue, NW
Washington, DC 20005
(202) 783-6868

National Clearinghouse for Alcohol and
Drug Information
P.O. Box 2345
Rockville, MD 20852
(301) 468-2600

National Committee for the Prevention of Alcoholism and Drug Dependency
6830 Laurel Street NW
Washington, DC 20012
(202) 723-4774

National Family Council Against Drug Abuse
40 Westminster Drive
Pearl River, NY 10965
(914) 735-9250

National Federation of Parents for Drug-Free Youth
8730 Georgia Avenue, Suite 200
Silver Spring, MD 20910
(301) 585-5437

National Listen America Club
2686 Townsgate Road
Westlake Village, CA 91359
(805) 497-9457

Drugs Anonymous
P.O. Box 473
Ansonia Station
New York, NY 10023
(212) 874-0700

Potsmokers Anonymous
316 East Third Street
New York, NY 10009
(212) 254-1777

Rubicon, Inc.
1300 MacTavish Avenue
Richmond, VA 23230
(804) 359-3255

Shepherd's Fold Ministries
1324 El Rancho Drive
Santa Cruz, CA 95060
(408) 423-4382

Alcoholism and Drug Abuse: Resources for Minorities

California Area Indian Health Service
2999 Fulton Avenue
Sacramento, CA 95821
(916) 978-4191

California Hispanic Commission on Alcohol and Drug Abuse
2400 O Street
Sacramento, CA 95816
(916) 443-5473

Division of Health Program Development
Indian Health Service
7900 South J Stock Road
Tucson, AZ 85746-9352
(612) 629-6703

Hispanic Health Council
96-98 Cedar Street
Hartford, CT 06106
(203) 527-0856

Nashville Area Indian Health Service
Oaks Tower Building, Suite 810
1101 Kermit Drive
Nashville, TN 37217-2191
(615) 736-5104, ext. 35

National Asian/Pacific Families against Substance Abuse
6303 Friendship Court
Bethesda, MD 20817
(301) 530-0945

National Association of Native American Children of of Alcoholics
P.O. Box 3364
Seattle, WA 98114
(206) 324-9360

National Black Alcoholism Council
417 South Dearborn Street, Suite 1000
Chicago, IL 60605
(312) 663-5780

National Coalition of Hispanic Health and Human Services Organization
1030 Fifteenth Street NW, Suite 1053
Washington, DC 20005
(202) 371-2100

National Hispanic Family against Drug Abuse
1511 K Street, Suite 1029
Washington, DC 20005
(202) 393-5136

Navajo Area Indian Health Service
P.O. Box G, Window Rock, AZ 86515
(612) 871-4811

Alcoholism and Drug Abuse: State Treatment Agencies

Alabama

Division of Mental Illness and Substance Abuse Community Programs
Department of Mental Health
200 Interstate Park Drive
P.O. Box 3710
Montgomery, AL 36193
(205) 271-9253

Alaska

Office of Alcoholism and Drug Abuse
Department of Health and Social Services
Pouch H-05-F
Juneau, AK 99811
(907) 586–6201

American Samoa

Social Services Division Alcohol and Drug Program
Government of American Samoa
Pago Pago, American Samoa 96799

Public Health Services
LBJ Tropical Medical Center
Pago Pago, American Samoa 96799

Arizona

Office of Community Behavioral Health
Department of Health Services
Alcohol Abuse and Alcoholism Section
701 East Jefferson Street, Suite 400A
Phoenix, AZ 85034
(602) 220–6478

Office of Community Behavioral Health
Department of Health Services
Drug Abuse Section
701 East Jefferson Street, Suite 400A
Phoenix, AZ 85034
(602) 255–1152

Arkansas

Office on Alcohol and Drug Abuse Prevention
Donaghey Plaza North, Suite 400
P.O. Box 1437
Little Rock, AR 72203-1437
(501) 682-6650

California

Department of Alcohol and Drug Programs
111 Capitol Mall, Suite 450
Sacramento, CA 95814
(916) 445-0834

Colorado

Alcohol and Drug Abuse Division
Department of Health
4210 East Eleventh Avenue
Denver, CO 80220
(303) 331-8201

Connecticut

Alcohol and Drug Abuse Commission
999 Asylum Avenue, Third Floor
Hartford, CT 06105
(203) 566-4145

Division of Alcoholism, Drug Abuse, and Mental Health
1901 North Dupont Highway
Newcastle, DE 19720
(302) 421-6101

District of Columbia

Office of Health Planning and Development
1875 Connecticut Avenue NW, Suite 836
Washington, DC 20009
(202) 673–7481

Florida

Alcohol and Drug Abuse Program
Department of Health and Rehabilitative Services
1317 Winewood Boulevard
Tallahassee, FL 32301
(904) 488–0900

Guam

Department of Mental Health and
Substance Abuse
P.O. Box 9400
Tamuning, Guam 96911
(671) 646–9262

Georgia

Alcohol and Drug Services Section
878 Peachtree Street NE, Suite 318
Atlanta, GA 30309
(404) 894–6352

Hawaii

Alcohol and Drug Abuse Branch
Department of Health
P.O. Box 3378
Honolulu, HI 96801
(808) 548–4280

Idaho

Bureau of Substance Abuse and Social Services
Department of Health and Welfare
450 West State Street, Seventh Floor
Boise, ID 83720
(208) 334-5935

Illinois

Department of Alcoholism and Substance Abuse
100 West Randolph Street, Suite 5-600
Chicago, IL 60601
(312) 917-3840

Indiana

Division of Addiction Services
Department of Mental Health
117 East Washington Street
Indianapolis, IN 46204
(317) 232-7816

Iowa

Department of Public Health
Division of Substance Abuse and Health Promotion
Lucas State Office Building, Fourth Floor
Des Moines, IA 50319
(515) 281-3641

Kansas

Alcohol and Drug Abuse Services
2700 West Sixth Street
Biddle Building
Topeka KS 66606-3925
(913) 296-3925

Kentucky

Division of Substance Abuse
Department of MH–MR Services
275 East Main Street
Frankfort, KY 40621
(502) 564–2880

Louisiana

Office of Prevention and Recovery from Alcohol and Drug Abuse
2744–B Woodale Boulevard
Baton Rouge, LA 70805
(504) 922–0730

Maine

Office of Alcoholism and Drug Abuse Prevention
Bureau of Rehabilitation
State House Station, Room 11
Augusta, ME 04333
(207) 289–2781

Maryland

State Drug Abuse Administration
201 West Preston Street
Baltimore, MD 21201
(301) 225–6925

Massachusetts

Division of Substance Abuse Services
150 Tremont Street
Boston, MA 02111
(617) 727–8614

Michigan

Office of Substance Abuse Services
Department of Public Health
3423 North Logan Street
Lansing, MI 48909
(517) 335-8809

Minnesota

Chemical Dependency Program Division
Department of Human Services
444 Lafayette Road
Saint Paul, MN 55155-3823
(612) 296-4610

Mississippi

Division of Alcohol and Drug Abuse
Department of Mental Health
Robert E. Lee Building, Eleventh Floor
Jackson, MS 39201
(601) 359-1288

Missouri

Division of Alcohol and Drug Abuse
Department of Mental Health
1915 South Ridge Drive, P.O. Box 687
Jefferson City, MO 65102
(314) 751-4942

Montana

Alcohol and Drug Abuse Division, State of Montana
Department of Institutions
Helena, MT 59601
(406) 444-2827

Nebraska

Division of Alcoholism and Drug Abuse
Department of Institutions
P.O. Box 94728
Lincoln, NE 68509
(402) 471-2851, ext. 5583

Nevada

Bureau of Alcohol and Drug Abuse
Department of Human Resources
505 East King Street
Carson City, NV 89710
(702) 885-4790

New Hampshire

Office of Alcohol and Drug Abuse Prevention
Health and Welfare Building
Hazen Drive
Concord, NH 03301
(603) 271-4627

New Jersey

Division of Alcoholism
129 East Hanover Street
Trenton, NJ 08625
(609) 292-8947

Division of Narcotic and Drug Abuse Control
129 East Hanover Street
Trenton, NJ 08625
(609) 292-5760

New Mexico

Substance Abuse Bureau
Behavioral Health Services Division
P.O. Box 968
Sante Fe, NM 87504-0968
(505) 827-0117

New York

Division of Alcoholism and Alcohol Abuse
194 Washington Avenue
Albany, NY 12210
(518) 474-5417

Division of Substance Abuse Services
Executive Park South
Box 8200
Albany, NY 12203
(518) 457-7629

North Carolina

Alcohol and Drug Section
Division of Mental Health and Mental Retardation Services
325 North Salisbury Street
Raleigh, NC 27611
(911) 733-4670

North Dakota

Division of Alcoholism and Drug Abuse
Department of Human Services
State Capitol Judicial Wing
Bismarck, ND 58505
(701) 224-2769

Ohio

Bureau of Alcohol Abuse and Recovery
Ohio Department of Health
170 North High Street, Third Floor
Columbus, OH 43266-0586
(614) 466-3445

Bureau on Drug Abuse
Ohio Department of Health
170 North High Street, Third Floor
Columbus, OH 43266-0586
(614) 466-7893

Oklahoma

Alcohol and Drug Programs
Department of Mental Health
P.O. Box 53277
Capitol Station
Oklahoma City, OK 73152
(405) 271-7474

Oregon

Office of Alcohol and Drug Abuse Programs
301 Public Service Building
Salem, OR 97310
(503) 378-2163

Pennsylvania

Office of Drug and Alcohol Programs
Department of Health
P.O. Box 90
Harrisburg, PA 17108
(717) 787-9857

Puerto Rico

Department of Anti-Addiction Services
P.O. Box B-Y
Rio Piedras Station
Rio Piedras, Puerto Rico 00928
(809) 764-3795

Rhode Island

Division of Substance Abuse
Substance Abuse Administration Building
Cranston, RI 02920
(401) 464-2091

South Carolina

Commission on Alcohol and Drug Abuse
3700 Forest Drive
Columbia, SC 29204
(803) 734-9520

South Dakota

Division of Alcohol and Drug Abuse
Joe Foss Building
523 East Capitol
Pierre, SD 57501
(605) 773-3123

Tennessee

Alcohol and Drug Abuse Services
Department of Mental Health and Mental Retardation
706 Church Street, Fourth Floor
Nashville, TN 37219
(615) 741-1921

Texas

Commission on Alcohol and Drug Abuse
1705 Guadalupe Street
Austin, TX 78701
(512) 463-5510

Trust Territories

Director of Health Services
Offices of the High Commissioner
Saipan, Trust Territories 96950
(615) 741-1921

Utah

Division of Substance Abuse
120 North 200 West, Fourth Floor
P.O. Box 45500
Salt Lake City, UT 84145-0500
(801) 538-3939

Vermont

Office of Alcohol and Drug Abuse Programs
103 South Maine Street
Waterbury, VT 05676
(802) 241-2170

Virginia

Office of Substance Abuse Services
Department of Mental Health and
Mental Retardation
P.O. Box 1797, 109 Governor Street
Richmond, VA 23214
(804) 786-3906

Virgin Islands

Division of Mental Health, Alcoholism,
and Drug Dependency
P.O. Box 520
Saint Croix, Virgin Islands 00820
(809) 773–1992

Washington

Bureau of Alcoholism and Substance Abuse
Department of Social and Health Service
Mail Stop OB–44W
Olympia, WA 98504
(206) 753–5866

West Virginia

Division of Alcohol and Drug Abuse, State Capitol
1800 Washington Street East, Room 451
Charleston, WV 25305
(304) 348–2276

Wisconsin

Office of Alcohol and Other Drug Abuse
1 West Wilson Street
P.O. Box 7851
Madison, WI 53707
(608) 266–3442

Wyoming

Alcohol and Drug Abuse Programs
Hathaway Building
Cheyenne, WY 82002
(307) 777–7115, ext. 7118

Alcoholism and Drug Abuse: State Departments of Rehabilitation

Alabama

Division of Rehabilitation
2129 East South Boulevard
P.O. Box 11586–0586
Montgomery, AL 36111
(205) 281–8780

Alaska

Division of Vocational Rehabilitation
Juneau, AK 99811
(907) 465–2814

American Samoa

Division of Rehabilitation
P.O. Box 3492, American Samoa Government
Pago Pago, American Samoa 96799

Arizona

Division of Rehabilitation Services
Department of Economic Security
1300 West Washington Street
Phoenix, AZ 85007
(602) 542–3332

Arkansas

Division of Rehabilitation Services
P.O. Box 3781, 1401 Brookwood Drive
Little Rock, AR 72203
(501) 371–2411

California

Department of Rehabilitation
830 K Street Mall,
Sacramento, CA 95814
(916) 445-3971

Colorado

Division of Rehabilitation Services
717 Seventeenth Street
P.O. Box 18-1000
Denver, CO 80218-0899
(303) 294-2804

Connecticut

Division of Rehabiliation Services
600 Asylum Avenue
Hartford, CT 06105
(203) 566-4440

Delaware

Division of Rehabilitation
Elwyn Building
321 East Eleventh Street
Wilmington, DE 19801
(302) 571-2851

District of Columbia

Rehabilitation Services Administration
605 G Street NW
Room 1101-E
Washington, DC 20001
(202) 727-3227

Florida

Division of Vocational Rehabilitation
Tallahassee, FL 32399-0696
(904) 488-6210

Georgia

Division of Rehabilitation Services
878 Peachtree Street NE, Room 706
Atlanta, GA 30309
(404) 894-6670

Guam

Department of Vocational Rehabilitation
Government of Guam
122 Harmon Plaza, Room B-201
Harmon Industrial Park, Guam 96911
011671-646-8840

Hawaii

Division of Vocational Rehabilitation
P.O. Box 339
Honolulu, HI 96809
(808) 548-4769

Idaho

Division of Vocational Rehabilitation
650 West State
Len B. Jordan Building, Room 150
Boise, ID 83720
(208) 334-3390

Illinois

Department of Rehabilitation Services
623 East Adams Street
Springfield, IL 62706
(217) 782-2093

Indiana

Division of Vocational Rehabilitation
251 North Illinois Street
P.O. Box 7083
Indianapolis, IN 46207-7083
(317) 232-1139

Iowa

Division of Vocational Rehabilitation Services
510 East Twelfth Street
Des Moines, IA 50319-0146
(515) 281-6731

Kansas

Rehabilitation Services
2700 West Sixth Street
Biddle Building
Topeka, KS 66606
(913) 296-3911

Kentucky

Office of Vocational Rehabilitation
Capitol Plaza Office Tower
Frankfort, KY 40601
(502) 564-4440

Louisiana

Division of Rehabilitation Services
P.O. Box 94371
1755 Florida Street
Baton Rouge, LA 70804
(504) 342–2285

Maine

Vocational Rehabilitation Services
32 Winthrop Street
Augusta, ME 04433
(207) 289–2266

Maryland

Division of Vocational Rehabilitation
200 West Baltimore Street
Baltimore, MD 21201
(301) 333–2294

Massachusetts

Rehabilitation Commission
20 Park Plaza, Eleventh Floor
Statler Office Building
Boston, MA 02116
(617) 727–2172

Michigan

Bureau of Rehabilitation
P.O. Box 30010
Lansing, MI 48909
(517) 373–3391

Minnesota

Division of Rehabilitation Services
390 North Robert Street, Fifth Floor
Saint Paul, MN 55101
(612) 296-1822

Mississippi

Vocational Rehabilitation Division
P.O. Box 1698
Jackson, MS 39205
(601) 354-6825

Missouri

Division of Vocational Rehabilitation
2401 East McCarty Street
Jefferson City, MO 65101
(314) 751-3251

Montana

Rehabilitative Services Division
P.O. Box 4210
Helena, MT 59604
(406) 444-2590

Nebraska

Division of Rehabilitation Services
301 Centennial Mall, Sixth Floor
Lincoln, NE 68509-5026
(402) 471-3652

Nevada

Rehabilitation Division
Capitol Complex
505 East King Street
Carson City, NV 89710
(702) 885-4470

New Hampshire

Division of Vocational Rehabilitation
101 Pleasant Street
Concord, NH 03301
(603) 271-3121

New Jersey

Division of Vocational Rehabilitation Services
John Fitch Plaza
Labor and Industry Building, Room 1005
Trenton, NJ 08625
(609) 292-7880

New Mexico

Division of Vocational Rehabilitation
604 West San Mateo Drive
Santa Fe, NM 87503
(505) 827-3511

New York

Office of Vocational Rehabilitation
New York State Department of Education
1 Commerce Plaza, Room 1907
Albany, NY 12234
(518) 474-2714

North Carolina

Division of Vocational Rehabilitation Services
P.O. Box 26053
620 North West Street
Raleigh, NC 27611
(919) 733-3364

North Dakota

Vocational Rehabilitation Services
State Capitol
Bismarck, ND 58505
(701) 224-2907

Ohio

Bureau of Vocational Rehabilitation
4656 Heaton Road
Columbus, OH 43229
(614) 438-1250

Oklahoma

Division of Rehabilitative Services
P.O. Box 25352
2409 North Kelly, RS No. 24
Oklahoma City, OK 73125
(405) 424-4311

Oregon

Division of Vocational Rehabilitation
2045 Silverton Road NE
Salem, OR 97310
(503) 378-3830

PENNSYLVANIA

Office of Vocational Rehabilitation
Labor and Industry Building, Seventh and Forster Streets
Harrisburg, PA 17120
(717) 787-5244

PUERTO RICO

Division of Vocational Rehabilitation
P.O. Box 1118
Hato Rey Station
Hato Rey, PR 00919
(809) 725-1792

RHODE ISLAND

Division of Vocational Rehabilitation
40 Fountain Street
Providence, RI 02903
(401) 421-7005

SOUTH CAROLINA

Department of Vocational Rehabilitation
P.O. Box 15
1410 Boston Avenue
West Columbia, SC 29171-0015
(803) 734-3500

SOUTH DAKOTA

Department of Vocational Rehabilitation
Division of Rehabilitative Services
700 Governor's Drive
Pierre, SD 57501
(605) 773-3195

Tennessee

Division of Rehabilitation
400 Deaderick Street
Citizens Plaza, Fifteenth Floor
Nashville, TN 37219
(615) 741-2019

Texas

Rehabilitation Commission
118 East Riverside Drive
Austin, TX 78704-9982
(512) 445-8108

Utah

Division of Rehabilitation Services
250 East 500 South
Salt Lake City, UT 84111
(801) 533-5991

Vermont

Vocational Rehabilitation Services
Waterbury Complex
103 South Main Street
Waterbury, VT 05676
(802) 241-2189

Virgin Islands

Division of Vocational Rehabilitation
Barbel Plaza South
Charlotte Amalie
St. Thomas, VI 00802
(809) 774-0930

Virginia

Department of Rehabilitative Services
P.O. Box 11045
Richmond, VA 23230-1045
(804) 257-0318

Washington

Division of Vocational Rehabilitation
Olympia, WA 98504
(206) 753-2544

West Virginia

Division of Vocational Rehabilitation
West Virginia Rehabilitation Center Institute
Charleston, WV 25305-0112
(304) 766-4600

Wisconsin

Division of Vocational Rehabilitation
P.O. Box 7852
1 West Wilson, Eighth Floor
Madison, WI 53707
(608) 266-1281

Wyoming

Division of Vocational Rehabilitation
326 Hathaway Building
Cheyenne, WY 82002-0710
(307) 777-7385

Battered Women/ Child Abuse Organizations

Abused Women's Aid in Crisis
G.P.O. Box 1699
New York, NY 10116
(212) 686-3628

Alcoholism Center for Women
1147 South Alvarado Street
Los Angeles, CA 90006
(213) 381-7805

Child Help U.S.A.
1345 El Centro Avenue
Hollywood, CA 90028
(213) 465-4016

Feminist Alliance against Rape
P.O. Box 21033
Washington, DC 20009
(202) 265-9262

House of Ruth
459 Massachusetts Avenue NW
Washington, DC 20001
(202) 842-0192

National Center for the Prevention and Control of Rape
U.S. Department of Health and Human Services
Room 15-99, Parklawn Building
Rockville, MD 20857
(301) 475-0257

National Coalition against Domestic Violence
P.O. Box 15127
Washington, DC 20003-0127
(202) 293-8860

National Domestic Violence Hotline
1-800-353-SAFE

National Organization for Victim Assistance
717 D Street NW
Washington, DC 20004
(202) 393-6682

Rape Crisis Center
P.O. Box 21005
Washington, DC 20009
(202) 333-7273

Women in Crisis (WIC)
133 West Twenty-first Street
New York, NY 10011
(212) 686-1942

Child Welfare Organizations/ Juvenile Justice

American Association of Children's Residential Centers
P.O. Box 14188
Washington, DC 20044
(202) 483-0605

American Association for Protecting Children
American Humane Association
9725 East Hampden Avenue
Denver, CO 80231
1-800-2-ASK-AHA

Big Brothers/Big Sisters of America
230 North Thirteenth Street
Philadelphia, PA 19107
(215) 567-7000

Catholic Big Brothers
1011 First Avenue
New York, NY 10022
(212) 371-1000

Child Welfare League of America
440 First Street NW
Washington, DC 20001
(202) 638-2952

Children's Advocacy Center
493 Sixty-second Street
Oakland, CA 94606
(415) 428-2273

Children's Defense Fund
1520 New Hampshire Avenue NW
Washington, DC 20036
(202) 483-1470

Children's Legal Rights Information and Training
2008 Hillyer Place NW
Washington, DC 20009
(202) 332-6575

Children's Rights, Inc.
3443 Seventeenth Street NW
Washington, DC 20010
(202) 462-7573

Clearinghouse on Child Abuse and Neglect Information
P.O. Box 1182
Washington, DC 20013
(703) 821-2086

Council for Exceptional Children
1920 Association Drive
Reston, VA 22091
(703) 620-3660

Daughters and Sons United
840 Guadalupe Parkway
San Jose, CA 95110
(408) 299-2475

International Society for Prevention of Child Abuse and Neglect
1205 Oneida Street
Denver, CO 80220
(303) 321-3963

Kempe Center for the Prevention and Treatment of Child Abuse and Neglect
1205 Oneida Street
Denver, CO 80220
(303) 321-3963

Legal Services for Children
149 Ninth Street
San Francisco, CA 94103
(415) 863-3762

National Association for Child Care Management
1255 Twenty-third Street NW, Suite 850
Washington, DC 20037
(202) 659-5955

National Black Child Development Institute
1463 Rhode Island Avenue NW
Washington, DC 20005
(202) 387-1281

National Center for Juvenile Justice
701 Forbes Avenue
Pittsburgh, PA 15219
(412) 227-6950

National Center for Missing and Exploited Children
Hotline: 1-800-621-4000

National Center for the Prevention and Treatment of Child Abuse and Neglect
University of Colorado Medical Center
1205 Oneida Street
Denver, CO 80220
(303) 321-3963

National Committee for Prevention of Child Abuse
332 South Michigan Avenue, Suite 950
Chicago, IL 60604
(312) 663-3520

National Consortium for Child Mental Health Services
3615 Wisconsin Avenue NW
Washington, DC 20016
(202) 966-7300

National Network of Youth Advisory Boards
P.O. Box 402036, Ocean View Branch
Miami Beach, FL 33140
(305) 532-2607

Parents United
P.O. Box 952
San Jose, CA 95108
(405) 280-5055

Society for Research in Child Development
University of Chicago Press
5720 Woodlawn Avenue
Chicago, IL 60637
(312) 702-7470

Employment/Vocational Education

American Youth Work Center
1522 Connecticut Avenue NW
Washington, DC 20036
(202) 785-0764

Legacy International Youth Program
111 South Patrick Street
Alexandria, VA 22314
(703) 549-3630

National Committee on Employment of Youth
1501 Broadway, Suite 1111
New York, NY 10036
(212) 840-1801

National Employment and Training Association
653 Eason Boulevard
Tupelo, MS 38801
(601) 842-5621

National Institute for Work and Learning
1200 Eighteenth Street NW, Suite 316
Washington, DC 20036
(202) 887-6800

National Office for Social Responsibility
222 South Washington Street
Alexandria, VA 22314
(703) 549-5304

National Youth Employment Coalition
1501 Broadway
New York, NY 10036
(212) 840-1801

70001 LTD
West Wing, Suite 300
600 Maryland Avenue SW
Washington, DC 20024
(202) 484-0103

Teen-Age Assembly of America
998 Ala Kapua Street
Honolulu, HI 96818
(808) 833-2422

Wildcat Service Corporation
660 First Avenue
New York, NY 10016
(212) 578-4940

Youth Development, Inc.
4575 Ruffner Street
San Diego, CA 92111
(619) 292-5683

Family Services

Ackerman Institute for Family Therapy
149 East Seventy-eighth Street
New York, NY 10021
(212) 879-4900

American Association for Marriage and Family Therapy
924 West Ninth Street
Upland, CA 91786
(714) 981-0888

American Family Therapy Association
1255 Twenty-third Street NW
Washington, DC 20037
(202) 659-7666

American Institute of Family Relations
5287 Sunset Boulevard
Los Angeles, CA 90027
(213) 465-5131

Association of Jewish Family and Children's Agencies
200 Park Avenue South, Sixth Floor
New York, NY 10003
(212) 674-6659

Emergency Council of Jewish Families
Two Penn Plaza, Suite 1500
New York, NY 10001
(212) 228-3100

Families in Action
P.O. Box 15053
Atlanta, GA 30333
(404) 378-3310

Families Anonymous
P.O. Box 344
Torrance, CA 90501
(213) 775-3211

Family Life Division
United States Catholic Conference
1312 Massachusetts Avenue NW
Washington, DC 20005
(202) 659-6672

Family Service America
11700 West Lake Park Drive
Milwaukee, WI 53224
(414) 359-2111

Institute for Family Research and Education
760 Ostrom Avenue
Syracuse, NY 13210
(315) 423-4584

Liberal Education for Adoptive Families
23247 Lofton Court North
Scandia, MN 55073
(612) 636-7031

Minorities Caucus of Family Service America
34½ Beacon Street
Boston, MA 02108
(617) 523-6400

Moviemento Familiar Cristiano
6932 Thrush Street
Houston, TX 77087
(713) 741-0658

National Alliance for Family Life
2025 I Street NW No. 306
Washington, DC 20006
(202) 659-2440

National Association of Jewish Family
Children's and Health Professionals
24123 Greenfield Street
Southfield, MI 48075
(313) 559-1500

National Conference on Parent Involvement
579 West Iroquois Street
Pontiac, MI 48053
(313) 334-5887

National Council on Family Relations
1219 University Avenue SE
Minneapolis, MN 55414
(612) 331-2774

National Forum of Catholic Parent Organizations
1077 Thirtieth Street NW
Washington, DC 20036
(202) 293-5954

National Institute of Marriage and Family Relations
6116 Rolling Road, Suite 306
Springfield, VA 22152
(703) 569-2400

Puerto Rican Family Institute
116 West Fourteenth Street
New York, NY 10011
(212) 924-6320

Step Family Foundation
333 West End Avenue
New York, NY 10023
(212) 877-3244

United Families of America
P.O. Box 6098
Arlington, VA 22206
(703) 527-6715

Family Planning and Sexuality

Alternatives to Abortion International
Hillcrest Hotel, Suite 511
Sixteenth and Madison Streets
Toledo, OH 43699
(419) 248-4471

American Institute of Family Relations (Sex Education)
5287 Sunset Boulevard
Los Angeles, CA 90027
(213) 465-5131

American Social Health Association (VD national hotline)
P.O. Box 13827
Research Triangle Park, NC 27709
(800) 227-8922

American Social Health Association
260 Sheridan Avenue, Suite 307
Palo Alto, CA 94306
(415) 321-5134

Catholics for a Free Choice
1411 K Street NW
Washington, DC 20005
(202) 638-1706

Center for Reproductive and Sexual Health
424 East Sixty-second Street
New York, NY 10021
(212) 758-7310

CHOICE
Women's Way
125 South Ninth Street, Suite 603
Philadelphia, PA 19107
(215) 592-7644

Citizens Alliance for VD Awareness
222 West Adams Street
Chicago, IL 60606
(312) 236-6339

Citizens Committee for Victim Assistance
53 West Jackson Street
Chicago, IL 60604
(312) 786-0500

Council for Sex Information and Education
P.O. Box 23088
Washington, DC 20024

E.C. Brown Foundation (Sex education)
300 Southwest Sixth Avenue
Portland, OR 97204
(503) 248-6931

Family Planning International Assistance
810 Seventh Avenue
New York, NY 10019
(212) 541-7800

Herpes Hotline
(919) 361–2120

Homosexual Information Center
6758 Hollywood Boulevard, Suite 208
Hollywood, CA 90028
(213) 464–8431

Human Life and Natural Family Planning Foundation
1511 K Street NW
Washington, DC 20005
(202) 393–1380

Infertility Associates
5530 Wisconsin Avenue, Suite 814
Chevy Chase, MD 20815
(301) 656–7577

Institute for Family Research and Education (Sex education)
760 Ostrom Avenue
Syracuse, NY 13210
(315) 423–4584

International Society of Reproductive Medicine (Fertility)
2960 West Eighth Street
Los Angeles, CA 90005
(213) 386–1970

National Abortion Federation
1436 U Street NW
Washington, DC 20009
(202) 687–5881

National AIDS Hotline
Centers for Disease Control
Atlanta, GA 30333
(800) 342–AIDS

National AIDS Information Clearinghouse
(301) 762-5111

National Association of Surrogate Mothers
8383 Wilshire Boulevard, Suite 750D
Beverly Hills, CA 90021
(213) 655-2015

National Family Planning and Reproductive Health Association
122 C Street NW, Suite 380
Washington, DC 20001
(202) 628-3535

National Gay and Lesbian Task Force
1517 U Street NW
Washington, DC 20009
(202) 332-6483

Operation Venus (Venereal disease)
1213 Clover Street
Philadelphia, PA 19107
(215) 567-6969

Federation of Parents and Friends of Lesbians and Gays
P.O. Box 20308
Denver, CO 80220
(303) 321-2270

Planned Parenthood Federation of America
810 Seventh Avenue
New York, NY 10019
(212) 541-7800

Planned Parenthood National Headquarters
810 Seventh Avenue
New York, NY 10019
(800) 223-3303

Premenstrual Syndrome Action
P.O. Box 16292
Irvine, CA 92713
(714) 854–4407

Sex Information and Education Council of the United States
32 Washington Place
New York, NY 10003
(212) 673–3850

Sexually Transmitted Diseases
The National Institute of Allergy and Infectious Diseases
Building 31, Room 7A32
Bethesda, MD 20205

U.S. Coalition for Life
P.O. Box 315
Export, PA 15632
(412) 327–7379

Disabilities

American Speech-Language-Hearing Association
10801 Rockville Pike
Rockville, MD 20852
(301) 897–5700

Association for Children and Adults with Learning Disabilities
4156 Library Road
Pittsburgh, PA 15234
(412) 341–1515

Council for Exceptional Children
1920 Association Drive
Reston, VA 22091
(703) 620–3660

National Council of Stutterers
c/o Speech and Hearing Clinic
Catholic University of America
Washington, DC 20064
(202) 635-5556

National Handicapped Sports and Recreation Association
1145 Nineteenth Street NW, Suite 717
Washington, DC 20036
(301) 652-7505

National Information Center for Handicapped Children and Youth
P.O. Box 1492
Washington, DC 20013
(703) 522-3332

Orton Society
1415 Bellona Lane, Suite 113
Towson, MD 21204
(301) 296-0232

Research and Demonstration Center for the Education of Handicapped Children and Youth
P.O. Box 223
Teachers College
Columbia University
New York, NY 10027
(212) 678-3873

Marriage and Divorce

American Association for Marriage and Family Therapy
924 West Ninth Street
Upland, CA 91786
(714) 981-0888

Children's Rights, Inc.
3443 Seventeenth Street NW
Washington, DC 20010
(202) 462-7573

National Association of Christian Marriage Counselors
P.O. Box 782
Terrell, TX 75160
(214) 563-1193

National Institutes of Marriage and Family Relations
6116 Rolling Road, Suite 316
Springfield, VA 22152
(703) 569-2400

Step Family Foundation
333 West End Avenue
New York, NY 10023
(212) 877-3244

Women Helping Women (Divorce)
c/o Ruth Kvalheim
525 North VanBuren Avenue
Stoughton, WI 53589
(608) 873-3747

Mental Health

Alfred Adler Institute
1841 Broadway
New York, NY 10023
(212) 974-0431

American Academy of Child and Adolescent Psychiatry
3615 Wisconsin Avenue NW
Washington, DC 20016
(202) 966-7300

American Anorexia/Bulimia Association, Inc.
133 Cedar Lane
Teaneck, NJ 07666
(201) 836-1800

American Association of Psychiatric Services for Children
1200-C Scottsdale Road, Suite 225
Rochester, NY 14624
(716) 235-6910

American Psychological Association
1200 Seventeenth Street NW
Washington, DC 20036
(202) 955-7600

American Society for Adolescent Psychiatry
5530 Wisconsin Avenue NW, Suite 1149
Washington, DC 20815
(301) 652-0646

Anorexia Bulimia Care, Inc.
P.O. Box 213
Lincoln Center, MA 01773
(617) 259-9767

Anorexia Nervosa and Related Eating Disorders, Inc.
P.O. Box 5102
Eugene, OR 97405
(503) 686-7372

Anorexics/Bulimics Anonymous
P.O. Box 112214
San Diego, CA 92111

Association for Child Psychoanalysis
c/o Moisy Shopper, M.D.
4524 Forest Park
St. Louis, MO 63108
(314) 361-4646

Association for Death Education and Counseling
638 Prospect Avenue
Hartford, CT 06105
(203) 232–4825

Behavior Therapy and Research Society
Henry Avenue
Eastern Pennsylvania Psychiatric Institute
Medical College of Pennsylvania
Philadelphia, PA 19129
(215) 475–9822

Community Guidance Service
133 East Seventy-third Street
New York, NY 10021
(212) 988–4800

Family Therapy Network
7703 Thirteenth Street NW
Washington, DC 20012
(202) 829–2452

Foundation for Better Living
201 East Eighty-seventh Street
P.O. Box 183, No. 8E
New York, NY 10128
(212) 860–2339

Karen Horney Clinic
329 East Sixty-second Street
New York, NY 10021
(212) 838–4333

National Association of Anorexia Nervosa and Associated Disorders
Box 7
Highland Park, IL 60035
(312) 831–3438

National Association of Social Workers
7981 Eastern Avenue
Silver Spring, MD 20901
(301) 565-0333

National Consortium for Child Mental Health Services
3615 Wisconsin Avenue NW
Washington, DC 20016
(202) 966-7300

National Mental Health Consumer Self-help Clearinghouse
311 South Juniper Street, room 902
Philadelphia, PA 19107
(215) 735-6367

National Sibling Network
5112 Fifteenth Avenue South
Minneapolis, MN 55417
(612) 872-1565

Schizophrenics Anonymous
1209 California Road
Eastchester, NY 10709
(914) 337-2252

World Association for Infant Psychiatry and
Allied Disciplines
Division of Child Psychiatry
Louisiana State University Medical Center
1542 Tulane Avenue
New Orleans, LA 70112
(504) 568-4451

Self-Help Groups

Adult Children of Alcoholics
P.O. Box 3216
2522 West Sepulveda Boulevard, Suite 200
Torrance, CA 90505
(213) 534-1815

Adults Molested as Children United
P.O. Box 952
San Jose, CA 95108
(408) 280–5055

Al-Anon Family Group Headquarters
One Park Avenue
New York, NY 10016
(212) 481–6565

Alcoholics Anonymous World Services
P.O. Box 459
Grand Central Station
New York, NY 10163
(212) 686–1100

Batterers Anonymous
P.O. Box 29
Redlands, CA 92373
(714) 793–7647

California Self-Help Center
405 Hilgard Avenue
University of California at Los Angeles
Los Angeles, CA 90024
(800) 222–LINK

Children of Alcoholics Foundation
200 Park Avenue
New York, NY 10166
(212) 351–2680

Co-Dependents Anonymous
P.O. Box 33577
Phoenix, AZ 85067
(602) 277–7991

Committee for Children (Sexual abuse)
172 Twentieth Avenue
Seattle, WA 98122
(206) 322–5050

Compassionate Friends (Bereaved families)
P.O. Box 3696
Oak Brook, IL 60522
(708) 990-0010

Drug Abuse Alternatives Center
2800 Cleveland Avenue, Suite 11
Santa Rosa, CA 95403
(707) 544-3295

Drugs Anonymous
P.O. Box 473
Ansonia Station
New York, NY 10023
(212) 874-0700

Emotional Health Anonymous
2420 San Gabriel Boulevard
Rosemead, CA 91770
(818) 573-5482

Families Anonymous, Inc.
P.O. Box 528
Van Nuys, CA 91408
(818) 989-7841

Fatherhood Project
c/o Bank Street College of Education
610 West 112th Street
New York, NY 10025
(212) 663-7200

Grandparents Anonymous (Custody)
1924 Beverly Street
Sylvan Lake, MI 48053
(313) 682-8384

Incest Survivors Resource Network International
P.O. Box 911
Hicksville, NY 11802
(516) 935-3031

International Society for Prevention of Child Abuse and Neglect
1205 Oneida Street
Denver, CO 80220
(313) 394–7576

Manic-Depressive Association
P.O. Box 4723
Stockton, CA 95204
(209) 951–1687

Mothers Against Drunk Driving (MADD)
669 Airport Freeway, Suite 310
Hurst, TX 76053
(817) 268–6233

Mothers Without Custody
P.O. Box 56762
Houston, TX 77256
(713) 840–1622

Nar-Anon Family Groups
P.O. Box 2562
Palos Verdes, CA 90274
(213) 547–5800

Narcotics Anonymous
P.O. Box 622
Sun Valley, CA 91352
(213) 764–3155

National Alliance for the Mentally Ill
11323 West Eighteenth Avenue
Lakewood, CO 80215
(303) 233–1750

National Association for Children of Alcoholics
31582 Coast Highway, Suite B
South Laguna, CA 92677
(714) 499–3889

National Self-Help Clearinghouse
Graduate School and University Center
33 West Forty-second Street
City University of New York
New York, NY 10036
(212) 840–7606

National Stuttering Project
656A Eighth Avenue
San Francisco, CA 94118
(415) 387–7065

National Women's Abuse Prevention Project
2000 P Street NW, Suite 508
Washington, DC 20036
(202) 857–0216

Overachievers Anonymous
1777 Union Street
San Francisco, CA 94123
(415) 928–3600

Overeaters Anonymous
2190 West 190th Street
Torrance, CA 90504
(213) 320–7941

Overspenders Anonymous
P.O. Box 23
A3 Quay Court
Sacramento, CA 95831

Parents Anonymous (Child abuse)
22330 Hawthorne Boulevard, Suite 208
Torrance, CA 90505
(213) 371–3501

Parents United
P.O. Box 952
San Jose, CA 95108
(405) 280-5055

Parents Without Partners
8807 Colesville Road
Silver Spring, MD 20910
(301) 588-9354

Pil-Anon Family Program
120 Gracie Square Station
New York, NY 10028
(212) 744-2020

Pills Anonymous
P.O. Box 473
Ansonia Station
New York, NY 10023
(212) 874-0700

Positives Anonymous World Services Office (AIDS)
25 Saint Marks Place
New York, NY 10003
(212) 732-6879

Potsmokers Anonymous
316 East Third Street
New York, NY 10009
(212) 254-1777

Remarried Parents, Inc.
c/o Jack Pflaster
102-20 Sixty-seventh Drive
Forest Hills, NY 11375
(718) 459-2011

Self-Help Center
1600 Dodge Avenue, Suite S-122
Evanston, IL 60201
(708) 328-0470

Self-Help Clearinghouse
St. Clares-Riverside Medical Center
Rocono Road
Denville, NJ 07834
(201) 625-7101

Sex Addicts Anonymous
P.O. Box 3038
Minneapolis, MN 55403
(612) 339-0217

Sexual Abuse Anonymous
(213) 432-7506

Shoplifters Anonymous International
Professional Building, Suite 300
202 Concord Road
Aston, PA 19014
(215) 497-2770

Smokenders, Inc.
Prospect Street at Route 22
Phillipsburg, NJ 08856
(201) 454-4357

Students Against Drunk Driving (SADD)
P.O. Box 800
Marlboro, MA 01752
(508) 481-3568

Survivors of Incest Anonymous
P.O. Box 21817
Baltimore, MD 21222-6817
(301) 282-3400

T-4 Anon (AIDS)
P.O. Box 10473
Kansas City, MO 64111
(816) 753-2774

ToughLove
P.O. Box 1069
Doyleston, PA 18901
(215) 348-7090

Victims Anonymous (Sexual abuse)
9514-0 Reseda Boulevard, no. 607
Northridge, CA 91324
(818) 993-1139

Voices in Action (Sexual abuse)
P.O. Box 148309
Chicago, IL 60614
(312) 327-1500

Wives Self-Help Foundation
8001 Roosevelt Boulevard
Smylie Times Building, Suite 202
Philadelphia, PA 19152
(215) 332-2311

Self-Help Groups: State Clearinghouses

Arizona

Rainy Day People Project
P.O. Box 472
Scottsdale, AZ 85252

California

California Self-Help Center
University of California at Los Angeles
405 Hilgard Avenue
Los Angeles, CA 90024
(800) 222-LINK

Northern Region Self-Help Center
Mental Health Association
5370 Elvas Avenue, Suite B
Sacramento, CA 95819
(916) 456-2070

Central Valley Self-Help Center
P.O. Box 343, Merced, CA 95341
(209) 723-8861

Southern Region Self-Help Center
Mental Health Association of San Diego
3958 Third Avenue
San Diego, CA 92103

Bay Area Self-Help Center, Mental Health Association
2398 Pine Street
San Francisco, CA 94115
(415) 921-4401

Self-Help Clearinghouse of Yolo County
Mental Health Association
P.O. Box 447, Davis, CA 95617
(916) 756-8181

Connecticut

Connecticut Self-Help/Mutual Support Network
Consultation Center
19 Howe Street
New Haven, CT 06511
(203) 789-7645

District of Columbia

Self-Help Clearinghouse of Greater Washington
Mental Health Association of Northern Virginia
100 North Washington Street, Suite 232
Falls Church, VA 22046
(703) 536-4100

Illinois

Self-Help Center
1600 Dodge Avenue, Suite S-122
Evanston, IL 60201
(312) 328–0470

Self-Help Center
Family Service of Champaign County
405 South State Street
Champaign, IL 61820
(217) 352–0092

Kansas

Self-Help Network
Campus Box 34
Wichita State University
Wichita, KS 67208–1595
(316) 689–3170

Massachusetts

Massachusetts Clearinghouse of Mutual Help Groups
Massachusetts Cooperative Extension
113 Skinner Hall
University of Massachusetts
Amherst, MA 01003
(413) 545–2313

Michigan

Michigan Self-Help Clearinghouse
109 West Michigan Avenue, Suite 900
Lansing, MI 48933
(517) 484–7373

Center for Self-Help
Riverwood Center
1485 Highway M–139
Benton Harbor, MI 49022
(616) 925–0594

Minnesota

Minnesota Mutual Help Resource Center
Wilder Foundation Community Care Unit
919 Lafond Avenue
Saint Paul, MN 55104
(612) 642–4060

Missouri

Support Group Clearinghouse
Kansas City Association for Mental Health
1020 East Sixty-third Street
Kansas City, MO 64110
(816) 561–HELP

Nebraska

Self-Help Information Services
1601 Euclid Avenue
Lincoln, NE 68502
(402) 476–9668

New Jersey

New Jersey Self-Help Clearinghouse
St. Clares-Riverside Medical Center
Denville, NJ 07834
(201) 625–9569

New York

Brooklyn Self-Help Clearinghouse
Heights Hills Mental Health Service
30 Third Avenue
Brooklyn, NY 11217
(718) 834-7341

Long Island Self-Help Clearinghouse
New York Institute of Technology
Central Islip Campus
Central Islip, NY 11722
(516) 348-3030

New York City Self-Help Clearinghouse, Inc.
P.O. Box 022812
Brooklyn, NY 11202
(718) 596-6000

New York State Self-Help Clearinghouse
New York Council on Children and Families
Empire State Plaza, Tower 2
Albany, NY 12224
(518) 474-6293

Westchester Self-Help Clearinghouse
Westchester Community College
Academics Arts Building
75 Grasslands Road
Valhalla, NY 10595
(914) 347-3620

Oregon

Northwest Regional Self-Help Clearinghouse
718 West Burnside Street
Portland, OR 97209
(503) 222-5555

Pennsylvania

Self-Help Group Network of the Pittsburgh Area
710½ South Avenue
Wilkensburg, PA 15221
(412) 247-5400

SHINE (Self-Help Information Network Exchange)
c/o Voluntary Action Center
225 North Washington Avenue
Park Plaza, Lower Level
Scranton, PA 18503
(717) 961-1234

Rhode Island

Support Group Helpline
Rhode Island Department of Health
Cannon Building
Davis Street
Providence, RI 02908
(401) 277-2223

South Carolina

Midland Area Support Group Network
Lexington Medical Center
2710 Sunset Boulevard
West Columbia, SC 29169
(803) 791-9227

Tennessee

Support Group Clearinghouse
Mental Health Association of Knox County
6712 Kingston Pike, No. 203
Knoxville, TN 37919
(614) 584-6736

Texas

Texas Self-Help Clearinghouse
Mental Health Association in Texas
1111 West Twenty-fourth Street
Austin, TX 78705
(512) 454-3706

Dallas Self-Help Clearinghouse
Mental Health Association of Dallas County
2500 Maple Avenue
Dallas, TX 75201-1998
(214) 871-2420

Self-Help Clearinghouse
Mental Health Association in Houston and Harris County
2211 Norfolk Street, Suite 810
Houston, TX 77098
(713) 523-8963

Greater San Antonio Self-Help Clearinghouse
Mental Health in Greater San Antonio
1407 North Main Street
San Antonio, TX 78212
(512) 222-1571

Tarrant County Self-Help Clearinghouse
Mental Health Association of Tarrant County
3136 West Fourth Street
Fort Worth, TX 76107-2113
(817) 335-5405

Vermont

Vermont Self-Help Clearinghouse
c/o Parents Assistance Line
103 South Main Street
Waterbury, VT 05676
(802) 241-2249

Social Welfare Organizations

Adoptees in Search
P.O. Box 41016
Bethesda, MD
(301) 656-8555

American Family Therapy Association
2020 Pennsylvania Avenue NW, Suite 273
Washington, DC
(202) 994-9000

American Foster Care Resources
P.O. Box 271
King George, VA 22485
(703) 775-7410

Association for Multicultural Counseling
and Development
c/o American Association for Counseling
and Development
5999 Stevenson Avenue
Alexandria, VA 22304
(703) 823-9800

Bereavement Center (Children)
Westchester Jewish Community Services
141 North Central Avenue
Hartsdale, NY 10530
(914) 949-6761

Big Brothers/Big Sisters of America
230 North Thirteen Street
Philadelphia, PA 19107
(215) 567-7000

Child Abuse Listening Mediation (Child welfare)
P.O. Box 90754
Santa Barbara, CA 93190
(805) 965-2376

Child Care Employee Project
(Employment)
P.O. Box 5603
Berkeley, CA 94705
(415) 653-9889

Child Welfare League of America
440 First Street NW, Suite 310
Washington, DC 20001
(202) 638-2952

ChildHelp U.S.A., Inc.
6463 Independence Avenue
Woodland Hills, CA 91370
(818) 347-7280

Committee for Mother and Child Rights
Route 1, P.O. Box 256A
Clear Brook, VA 22624
(703) 722-3652

Committee for Single Adoptive Parents
P.O. Box 15084
Chevy Chase, MD 20815
(202) 966-6367

Division for the Physically Handicapped
(Children
c/o Council for Exceptional Children
1920 Association Drive
Reston, VA 22091
(703) 620-3660

E.C. Brown Foundation (Families)
101 Southwest Main Street, Suite 500
Portland, OR 97204
(503) 275-9512

Emerge: A Men's Counseling Service on
Domestic Violence
280 Green Street
Second Floor
Cambridge, MA 02139
(617) 547-9870

Family Planning National Clearinghouse
P.O. Box 12921
Arlington, VA 22209
(703) 558-7923

Family Resource Coalition
230 North Michigan Avenue
Room 1625
Chicago, IL 60601
(312) 726-4750

Family Service America
11700 West Lake Park Drive
Milwaukee, WI 53224
(414) 359-2111

Foster Grandparents Program
1100 Vermont Avenue NW
Room 6100
Washington, DC 20525
(800) 424-8580

Haitian and Co-Arts Association
(Child welfare)
165 Park Row
Suite 8D
New York, NY 10038
(212) 732-9735

International Child Resource Institute
1810 Hopkins Street
Berkeley, CA 94707
(415) 644-1000

International Society for Prevention of Child Abuse and Neglect
1205 Oneida Street
Denver, CO 80220
(303) 321-3963

Interracial Family Alliance
P.O. Box 16248
Houston, TX 77222
(713) 454-5018

Interracial-Intercultural Pride (Families)
1060 Tennessee Street
San Francisco, CA 94107

Joint Custody Association
10606 Wilkins Avenue
Los Angeles, CA 90024
(213) 475-5352

Missing Children Help Center
410 Ware Boulevard, Suite 400
Tampa, FL 33619
(813) 623-5437

National Association of Counsel for Children
1205 Oneida Street
Denver, CO 80220
(303) 321-3963

National Coalition against Domestic Violence
P.O. Box 15127
Washington, DC 20003
(202) 293-8860

National Coalition to End Racism in America's
Child-Care System
22075 Koths Street
Taylor, MI 48180
(313) 295-0257

National Council on Child Abuse and Family Violence
1155 Connecticut Avenue NW, Suite 400
Washington, DC 20036
(202) 429-6695

National Council for Children's Rights
2001 O Street NW
Washington, DC 20036
(202) 223-NCCR

National Exchange Club Foundation for the Prevention of
Child Abuse
3050 Central Avenue
Toledo, OH 43606
(419) 535-3232

National Legal Resource Center for Child Advocacy
and Protection
1800 M Street NW, Second Floor South
Washington, DC 20036
(202) 331-2250

Organized Adoption Search Information Services
P.O. Box 53-0761
Miami Shores, FL 33153
(305) 945-2758

PACE: Parents and Children's Equality (Divorce)
1816 Florida Avenue
Palm Harbor, FL 34683
(813) 787-3875

Parents Sharing Custody
435 North Bedford Drive, Suite 310
Beverly Hills, CA 90210
(213) 273-9042

Save the Children Federation
54 Wilton Road
Westport, CT 06880
(203) 226-7271

Task Force on Families in Crisis
4004 Hillsboro Road, Suite 223B
Nashville, TN 37215
(615) 383-4575

The Youth Project (Community organization)
2335 Eighteenth Street NW
Washington, DC 20009
(202) 483-0030

Youth Resources

A Better Chance (Exceptional minority students)
334 Boylston Street
Boston, MA 02116
(617) 536-5270

Alcohol Education for Youth
1500 Western Avenue
Albany, NY 12203
(518) 456-3800

Allied Youth and Family Counseling Center
310 North Windemere Street
Dallas, TX 75208
(214) 943-1044

American Field Society (AFS)
International/Intercultural Programs
313 East Forty-third Street
New York, NY 10017
(212) 661-4550

American Society for Adolescent Psychiatry
24 Green Valley Road
Wallingford, PA 19086
(215) 566-1054

Boys Club Professional Association
c/o Mary Ann Christiansen
P.O. Box 4306
Denver, CO 80204
(303) 893-2600

Center for Women's Studies and Services
908 East Street
San Diego, CA 92101
(714) 233-8984

Children of the Night (Runaways)
P.O. Box 4343
Hollywood, CA 90078
(213) 461-3160

City Kids Foundation
57 Leonard Street
New York, NY 10013
(212) 925-3320

Covenant House Nineline (24-Hour crisis intervention)
440 Ninth Avenue
New York, NY 10001
(800) 999-9999

Direction Sports
117 West Ninth Street, Suite 520
Los Angeles, CA 90015
(213) 627–9861

Encampment for Citizenship (Multiracial government model)
2 West Sixty-fourth Street
New York, NY 10023
(212) 787–2714

4-H Program
SEA/Extension
U.S. Department of Agriculture
Washington, DC 20250
(202) 447–5853

Girls Incorporated
30 East Thirty-third Street
New York, NY 10016
(212) 689–3700

Help, Inc. (Peer counseling)
638 South Street
Philadelphia, PA 19147
(215) 546–7766

I Have a Dream Foundation (Scholarships)
330 Seventh Avenue
New York, NY 10001
(212) 736–1730

Institute in Basic Youth Conflicts
P.O. Box 1
Oak Brook, IL 60522
(312) 323–9800

National Anorexia Aid Society
5796 Karl Road
Columbus, OH 43229
(614) 436–1112

National Association of Girls Clubs
5808 Sixteenth Street NW
Washington, DC 20011
(202) 726-2044

National Black Youth Leadership Council
250 West Fifty-fourth Street, Suite 800
New York, NY 10019
(212) 541-7600

National Center for Youth Law
1663 Mission Street
San Francisco, CA 94103
(415) 543-3307

National Commission on Resources for Youth
36 West Forty-fourth Street
New York, NY 10036
(212) 840-2844

National Committee on Youth Suicide Prevention
825 Washington Street
Norwood, MA 02062
(617) 769-5686

National Listen America Club
2686 Townsgate Road
Westlake Village, CA 91359
(805) 497-9457

National Runaway Switchboard and Suicide Hotline
3080 North Lincoln Avenue
Chicago, IL 60657
(800) 621-4000

Operation Sisters United (Teenage girls of color)
1104 Allison Street NW
Washington, DC 20011
(202) 659-0006

Suicide Prevention Center of Los Angeles
1041 South Menlo Avenue
Los Angeles, CA 90006
(213) 386-5111

Teen-Age Assembly of America (Overcoming delinquency)
998 Ala Kapua Street
Honolulu, HI 96818
(808) 933-2422

Youth of All Nations
16 Saint Lukes Place
New York, NY 10014
(212) 924-1358

Youth American Red Cross
Programs and Services
Seventeenth and D Streets NW
Washington, DC 20006
(202) 737-8300

Youth Counseling League
138 East Nineteenth Street
New York, NY 10003
(212) 473-4300

Youth Development, Inc. (Runaway shelters)
4575 Ruffner Street
San Diego, CA 92111
(619) 292-5683

Youth Suicide National Center
445 Virginia Avenue
San Mateo, CA 94402
(415) 347-3961

Young Men's Christian Association (YMCA) Program Services
356 West Thirty-fourth Street, Suite 377
New York, NY 10001
(212) 563-3471

Young Women's Christian Association (YWCA) of the United States of America
726 Broadway
New York, NY 10003
(212) 614-2700

About the Authors

SCOTT O. HARRIS, Ph.D., attended the University of Michigan and performed graduate work in human development at the University of Chicago. He completed a second master's degree in clinical psychology and a doctorate in clinical psychology at the California School of Professional Psychology in Los Angeles. He is a licensed clinical psychologist in private practice in West Los Angeles, California. Having formerly served as chief psychologist at a child-guidance clinic and on staff at Children's Hospital in San Francisco, he is currently on staff with Managed Health Network, a national managed mental-health care company. A large portion of Dr. Harris's practice is devoted to working with teenagers, but he also provides services to adults and children. Dr. Harris is a consultant to several private high schools as well as to the film and television industries.

EDWARD N. REYNOLDS, Ph.D., was born in the college community of Oberlin, Ohio and graduated from Oberlin College. He completed graduate work, initially in psychiatric social work, and later in psychology, at Case Western Reserve University. He also completed a period of postdoctoral study at Brandeis University under the direction of the late Abraham H. Maslow, Ph.D., one of the pioneers of humanistic psychology. Dr. Reynolds has taught at a number of institutions of higher learning including Kent State University, Boston College, and the California School of Professional Psychology. Since 1979 he has been in private practice as a clinical psychologist working with adolescents, adults, and families. He maintains offices in Los Angeles and San Diego.